From Idealism to Realism:
A 25 YEAR ODYSSEY

Barry J. Konovitch

From Idealism to Realism:
A 25 YEAR ODYSSEY

Barry J. Konovitch

KTAV Publishing House, Inc.
Hoboken, New Jersey

Copyright © 1993
Barry J. Konovitch

Library of Congress Cataloging-in-Publication Data

Konovitch, Barry J.
    From idealism to realism : a 25 year odyssey / Barry J. Konovitch.
        p.   cm.
    ISBN 0-88125-465-7
    1. Jewish sermons, American. 2. Jews--Civilization. 3. Israel-
-History. 4. Judaism--United States. 5. Jews--United States.
6. United States--Ethnic relations. I. Title.
BM740.2.K635 1993
296.4'2--dc20   93-19757
                                                                            CIP

Manufactured in the United States of America

*Dedicated to my good friends
Alfred and Sayde Swire,
whose lives are dedicated to
scholars and scholarship.*

Contents

PART III
The Jewish Defense League

PART IV
The Odyssey of Soviet Jewry

PART V
Art, Music and Politics

PART VI
Digging Up the Past: Biblical Archaeology

PART VII
Sports: A Ticket to the Mainstream

PART VIII
The New Generation

PART IX
Blacks, Jews and other Minorities

Acknowledgments

I would like to acknowledge the people who encouraged and supported the writing of this book: My wife, Aileen, whose wisdom and courage inspires me and whose strength amazes me; my son Jonathan and daughter Jordanna who share my adventures and my dreams; my parents, Saba Si and Sabta Sarah, the Rabbi and Rebbetzin who pioneered the trail and pointed the way; and the members of my congregations who became our friends and supporters.

The Prologue: "The Times They Are A-changing"

History is by its very nature subjective; the moment an event is recorded it takes on the interpretation of the recorder and no two people see the same thing with the same eyes or with the same mind. Furthermore the same event takes on new shades of meaning with the passage of time, and even the extraneous occurrences of a particular day color recollections and interpretations. A disturbing encounter or a poor meal can have a subconscious but significant effect, not only on the present but on the recollected past. Those images that "flash across the inner eye" must be placed in the subjective context of "whose eye" and "what cinder is irritating it," Wordsworth notwithstanding. Therefore a rabbinic "remembrance of things past" flows from "right here and right now." Yesterday would have brought a different interpretation, and tomorrow yet another.

When I left the yeshiva 25 years ago I was prepared with the requisite scholarship to receive *semicha* (ordination). But I was not prepared to be a community rabbi in any contemporary sense. I had no degree in political science or international relations. I knew little about public relations and diplomacy or how to be an executive director, or fundraiser. I had never even performed a wedding or attended to a burial, or given a sermon. All these things would have to be learned, by trial and error.

My "practical rabbinics" training consisted of a course in homiletics and a field visit to a slaughter house, the essential difference being the victim of the knife; in the latter case the cow, and in the former the student. The pre-holocaust European Yeshiva with its brilliant Talmudic scholars and rigorously logical method may have been transplanted onto American shores but 25 years ago it had yet to come to terms with the

1

nature of American Jewish life in the second half of the twentieth century.

Fortunately I was blessed with parents and grandparents whose life's work was also the active rabbinate and who constituted a veritable laboratory of practical rabbinics. Actually I was the fourth generation in a line of rabbis, and I always attributed my choice of profession to a non-quantifiable genetic-historical imperative. Why else would a Jewish boy enter the Rabbinate, to paraphrase the old joke.

Scholarship is the sine qua non of the rabbinate and teaching is its raison d'être, yet we all remember from our university days that a brilliant mind with a wealth of knowledge does not automatically make an effective teacher. The art of communication makes the difference between pedantry and inspiration. And one should never minimize the effectiveness of teaching by example. The essential commandments that deal with interpersonal behavior that are all too often minimized or overlooked are best taught and reinforced by personal example. But the role of exemplar is difficult. The Rabbi and his family are exposed to the scrutiny of the entire community. To remain civil and even pleasant requires the patience of a saint, which is probably why there are no saints in Jewish history, only human beings of flesh and blood with feelings and emotions. Shakespeare had it right when he put those anguished words into Shylock's mouth: "If you prick us do we not bleed . . . if you poison us do we not die and if you wrong us shall we not revenge."

The rabbi is the authority figure in the Jewish community, and as with all authority figures he is occasionally the focus of rebellion. The man who sets standards and limits for human behavior as specified by the Torah had better be prepared for the "slings and arrows." Rabbinical seminary should provide a suit of armor along with a degree (and I don't mean only *tzizit*) for without a thick hide casualties will be suffered.

The congregant who suffered a loss may unconsciously hold G-d accountable, and who is the Lord's emissary on earth but the Rabbi. Sickness and death, family problems and economic hardship are often laid at the Rabbi's door. The correct incantation was not made, the right magic was not performed. It is the nature of a human being to blame anyone but himself.

More than two thousand years ago our ancestors developed the institution of the scapegoat whereby the sins and difficulties of the people were symbolically transferred to a goat that was dashed to pieces on the rocks of the Judean desert. The institution persists; only the goat has changed.

Rabbis are often lightning rods for the storms of the Jewish community. From the beginning of our history disagreements all too frequently took on the aspect of warfare. To avoid conflict pulpit rabbis may be forced into the "pareve mode" whereby each and every opinion offered or pronouncement made is considered solely on the basis of its potential for controversy. A blandness begins to pervade this kind of rabbinic offering, lacking salt and pepper and exhibiting the consistency of pablum. Platitudes replace precision, verbosity substitutes for originality and style is confused with substance. Everything is evaluated according to the standard of "politically correct."

An inordinate amount of time and energy is spent, nay wasted, on maintaining a political position instead of carrying out the true mandate of the rabbi as teacher, exemplar and mentor. Perhaps Moses may serve us as the archetypal rabbi, prodding and pulling a recalcitrant people, attempting to teach and convince a stubborn unyielding populace, suffering abuse and complaint, threats and intimidation, ultimately relegating one congregation to a desert grave in favor of a younger, more open minded and pliant one. In the process Moses loses his own family to the unreasonable demands of his people; he fails to achieve his fondest goal; he dies unappreciated; his grave is unmarked; his life is a tragedy that no amount of subsequent religious or historical fame can erase.

As long as synagogues are measured solely in terms of square footage, mortgage payments, membership size, and dues structures, instead of religiosity, humaneness, and downright "mentchlichkeit," the concept of holiness will elude us and our ancient purpose will remain perverted.

Twenty–five years ago the mainstays of the American traditional synagogue were men and women who respected the rabbi because he represented the accumulated wisdom of the Torah. It was an attitude transplanted from Europe; it had not yet been diluted by a secular American society. Today it is difficult to distinguish between a synagogue and a business, as the bottom line becomes the focus of energy.

Is the synagogue to be measured purely in quantitative terms or are we "in business" for a higher purpose? And is the Rabbi merely a chief executive officer whose effectiveness may be measured in dollar signs and decimal points? No one can dispute the fact that all institutions need financial support to flourish, but neither can we dispute the fact that financial support is the means to an end, not the end itself. In the last analysis we will stand or fall on the basis of how much "Yiddishkeit" we teach, how many Zionists we inspire and how many people we influence to lead a better, more Jewish life.

In recent years the newest generation of young Jews has exhibited a renewed interest in our spiritual heritage. They seem to be in search of that "authentic" Jewish experience, or at least a Judaism that can address itself in logical, coherent, and relevant terms to the problems and concerns of contemporary society. This "awakening" presents an opportunity and a challenge to Rabbis and teachers. The alarming rise in assimilation, prompted by indifference, aided and abetted by ignorance, and encouraged by the open society, can be slowed if not reversed by taking advantage of this small but significant phenomenon.

I have every confidence that we shall rise to the occasion, and the next twenty-five years will see a renaissance of Jewish life in America. However it will require the marshalling of the full resources of the Jewish community, both financial and intellectual, the prioritizing of quality Jewish education and the working partnership of rabbis, teachers, leaders, and parents. I cannot conceive of a more important agenda for the next century.

PART I
ISRAEL STANDS ALONE

Israel: A Land and a People

For the time being, the extremely volatile issue of who is to be officially considered a Jew has been settled. The law clearly defines a Jew as the offspring of a Jewish mother, or a convert to the faith. Last year's high court ruling has thus been overturned, reinforcing the ancient halachic hold over the Jewish people in Israel, as well as pointing a very definite course for Jews in the diaspora.

However, the parliament also granted full rights of citizenship to non-Jewish members of mixed marriages emigrating to Israel. The ruling comes at a time when Israel is fighting for the release of thousands of Soviet Jews, many in mixed families who wish to come to their national homeland.

So the Shalit children are not Jewish but are entitled to full rights as Israeli citizens.

But the issue is not really "Who is a Jew," but, as the London Sunday Telegraph put it, "what is Israel?" Is the modern state of Israel the re-established state that was destroyed by Titus 1900 years ago, or is it just another one of the newly founded post World War II states like Ghana or Indonesia. Is it the state to which the children of Abraham, Isaac and Jacob are returning or is it a 20th century phenomenon, a new nationality?

Obviously there can be no return for those who were never exiled. The exiles that left Israel 19 centuries ago took the Torah with them as their portable homeland, as their assurance of return, as their deed and writ of inheritance to the land. The Torah was their family record connecting them with their ancestors.

And yet with extraordinary liberality the House of Israel accepted as members those who entered through one of two doors: blood relationship through descent from a Jewish mother, or through moral commitment to the faith. The Shalit children, by decision of their father, refused to enter into the

7

Jewish nation through either door. Yet they have demanded to be accepted as Jews. Their demand implies that the House of Israel be separated from the people of the State of Israel. This new implication would mean that Israel is a new state, not conceived in the womb of Jewish history, Jewish thought and Torah.

The only people who could be happy about such a decision would be the Canaanites on the one hand, and the Neturei Karta and the Satmar Hasidim on the other. The only people who can benefit from such a decision would be the enemies of the state, those spiritually antagonistic to it, and those physically antagonistic to it.

Finally consider that at this moment there are thousands of Jewish youngsters around the world contemplating intermarriage against the will of their parents, parents who are ill-equipped to carry on their end of the debate. What can parents retort when their offspring quote the Supreme Court of Israel to the effect that one can marry out of the faith and still be accepted as a good Jew? What can be said to the scores of rabbis, teachers and communal leaders who may throw up their hands in disgust, and ask, "For this we need an Israel?"

It is time to reaffirm with all our power the bond between the land and the people of Israel.

Israel at Forty: Still Fighting for Survival

In recent months we have witnessed an Arab uprising in Judea, Samaria and Gaza. What began as riots has now turned into a war, a war even more serious than 1967 or 1973. During the "Six-Day War" and during the Yom Kippur War we faced tanks and jet-fighters, machine guns and grenades. The Israeli Defense Force (IDF) knows exactly how to deal with such weapons. But they do not know to deal with women and children. They were not trained to kill civilians, even those throwing rocks and bottles; even those who were responsible for ambushing a bus load of children in the Galil, even those who killed a 15-year-old girl in Beita and tried to kill all the youngsters with her.

The Palestinians have discovered the soft underbelly of Israel: We are unable to conduct ourselves as barbarians, even in times of war, even when our own lives are imperiled. (And I hope that the Israelis will forgive me for using "we," thereby including myself and all Jews. Because I too suffer their anguish, I feel their pain, I bleed with them; and if they fall, we all fall.) How does the strongest, most highly motivated army in the Middle East fight women and children? Far be it for us to suggest strategies sitting in the relative safety of America. But we have learned something from our own experiences in South East Asia and in Central America. In order to win a war you need to play by the rules of the particular war, and in the Middle East the rules of war dictate that children be sent to the front line, and that stones be used as weapons. How many children have died in the war between Iraq and Iran? How many people are executed by stoning in the Arab world?

Arab civilians, women and children included, may not be dressed in uniform, but when they hold a molotov cocktail or

9

a rock in their hands they are as dangerous and threatening as any soldier and they should be treated as such.

Should a Jew be afraid to walk in the streets of Israel? After 2,000 years of cringing before every uplifted fist do we not deserve the right to live peacefully and securely in at least one country in the world?

We welcome the Arabs in Israel to live in peace with us; to join us in the building of the land. Together we can turn the entire area into a "garden of prosperity." But if Israel does not meet with their approval, if the sight of a Jewish neighbour is too disturbing, if their standard of living is still not high enough, then they are free to live in one of the twenty-two other Arab States.

And if an Arab raises his stone-filled fist to crush a Jewish skull then he sends us a clear, life-threatening message, a message as deadly as any bullet. If we wish to defend ourselves, then the response must be quick and without hesitation; and it must come from the barrel of gun. To deal with the situation in any other way is to put ourselves in a defenseless situation, one that only encourages the terrorizing Palestinians to become bolder, more audacious, and more dangerous with each passing day.

The Palestinian Arabs can take up the plough or the molotov cocktail, the briefcase or the rock. The choice is theirs; but they must take full responsibility for their actions.

We invite the Arabs to live anywhere in Israel in peace. In the Galil, in Jerusalem, in Yehuda, in Shomron; in an Israel whose borders have been clearly defined by the Bible, by history and even by the League of Nations; not by wars and occupation. Those borders certainly include Hebron and Shechem, Judea and Samaria. If this historical fact is unacceptable, then Arab-Palestinians are free to join their Palestinian brothers in Jordan, a State artificially created especially for them by the British in 1924 out of land originally promised as part of the "Jewish Homeland." We have already given up enough land to the Arab-Palestinians without any peace in return.

And if there are American Jews who feel uncomfortable with the idea of Israelis defending their country and their lives, then

I suggest they keep their discomfort off the front pages of our newspapers. Now is a time for all Jews to rally behind the State of Israel, to offer our moral and financial support, to realize that Israel is fighting a war, and to understand that a secure Israel must be maintained at all costs. By their own admission the Palestinian Arabs would not even be satisfied with Judea and Samaria; they insist on Jerusalem, Haifa and Tel-Aviv. They look forward to the day when the Israelis are eliminated entirely from the Middle East, allowing the area to sink back into its levantine stupor. If some American Jews cannot or will not understand this, then at least be quiet instead of being foolish.

2,000 years ago, during the lengthy Roman occupation of Israel, Rabbi Akiva and Rabbi Yochanan Ben Zakkai could not agree on a plan of action.

The hawks counseled revolt; the doves counseled accommodation. When the political opportunities arose, Ben-Zakkai hesitated to ask for an independent Israel; instead he saved the university at Yavneh and its Torah scholars. To his dying day, he was haunted by Akiva's reprimand and fearful that he had not done enough to save the State. If the great Rabbi was fearful, should we not also be fearful? Should we not carefully weigh our words and our actions, for one day each and every one of us will be held responsible.

With Rabbi Akiva, we realize the importance of Israel and the need to fight for its existence; to let nothing and no one stand in the way of Israel's security. With all the great rabbis of all generations we believe in "The People of Israel, with the Torah of Israel, in the Land of Israel."

This is a time of testing for all Jews and for freedom-loving people around the world. Are you proud enough, strong enough, and wise enough to pass the test?

Stand in solidarity with Israel as she celebrates 40 years of statehood.

Long live the State of Israel!

Controversy in Silwan: The Return to David's Jerusalem

The "old city" of Jerusalem, the one surrounded by the ancient walls and entered by those imposing gates, is not the oldest city of Jerusalem. The site of King David's capital lies to the south of the Dung Gate on a hill called the Ophel Ridge. It was here, in the present village known as Silwan, that a group of loosely federated Israelite tribes united to become a powerful nation. Even the present Arabic name for the area, "Silwan," is taken from the ancient Hebrew name for the main water reservoir at the foot of David's city, the "Shiloach pool."

The Ophel Ridge (Silwan) remained part of the walled city of Jerusalem for one thousand years, ruled over by the famous kings of Israel: Solomon, Hezekiah, Zedekiah, Simon the Hasmonean, and Herod the Great. When the Romans destroyed Judean Jerusalem and built Aelia Capitolina on its site, the City of David ridge was excluded for strategic reasons and quickly deteriorated in its abandonment.

Through several seasons of excavation at the City of David I have uncovered the floor of an Israelite house built circa 700 BCE; I have held in my hand the remains of a cooking jar used by our Israelite ancestors, circa 900 BCE; and I have laboriously helped to exposed the huge glacis-like structure that once formed the foundation of King David's fortress. For those who prefer to dismiss the Biblical deed to Jerusalem (and I am not one of them), the science of archaeology offers irrefutable evidence: The city of Jerusalem has been Israelite for 3,000 years. The only other people who can claim an earlier ownership is the Canaanite tribe known as the Jebusites. If there are any Jebusites alive in the world let them come forward and present their credentials and establish their claim. In their absence, the earliest legitimate claimants to the city are the Jewish people.

In 1888, as part of the "BILU" migration to Israel, a number of Yemenite families pioneered the return to King David's Jerusalem. They settled in Kfar Hashiloach, next to the Arabs of Silwan, who were recent immigrants to the area from the Arabian desert. In 1929 and again in 1936 these Jewish settlers were attacked by Arab rioters. Eventually the Jews had to abandon their homes and move to safer parts of Jerusalem. The Arabs of Silwan took over their houses, their property and whatever belongings were left behind. No protests were heard. No one demanded that Jewish rights be protected; not the British mandate authorities, not the United States, not the League of Nations.

In 1991 a handful of Jewish settlers moved back to their City of David. In an effort to be scrupulously fair, they purchased the houses from Arab "owners"—those same families who had chased out the Jewish owners some 62 years before. This reflected the precedent of King David, who purchased a piece of land in this area from Arauna the Hittite in order to establish uncontested ownership, even in his own homeland, for the future site of the Temple.

Those same governments who were so quiet when Jews were massacred and dispossessed by marauding Arabs in 1929 were the first ones to raise a hue and cry against these Israeli settlers. Ignored was the fact that Jerusalem is the 3,000 year old capital of Israel. Ignored was the fact that the question of legal ownership was carefully considered by the courts and clearly defined by the law. It takes a great deal of audacity, insensitivity and ignorance of history to attempt to dictate to Jewish people where they may live and not live in their own capital city. But the United Nations has no shortage of ignorance and insensitivity, having used stronger language in resolutions against Israel than even against Saddam Hussein's invasion of Kuwait.

The Israeli government is under no moral or legal obligation to recognize any Arab claim of ownership that is based at best on the rights granted by the Turkish occupational powers or the British mandate authorities, or at worst on pillage, rape and murder. Yet it goes out of its way to consider the needs of the Arab population and accords them equal protection under the law. If the Karáin of Silwan wish to contest ownership then they may do so in the courts. But for the moment it appears that the Jewish settlers in Silwan are in full compliance with the law. After 2,000 years they have returned home, and no amount of sanctimonious noise from foreign capitals will evict them. King David's spirit may now rest in peace.

A View from the Golan
November 7, 1991

The Seventh Armored Brigade is headquartered atop the Golan Plateau. During the Yom Kippur war a handful of Israeli Centurion tanks held off a huge column of Syrian armor and literally saved the Galilee from annihilation. The heroic Israeli commander whose courage and skill brought about the miraculous victory ultimately became the first Yemenite general in the history of the State. Avigdor Kahalani's picture hangs on the wall at headquarters along with a dozen illustrious brigade commanders who constitute a veritable "who's who" of famous Israeli personalities.

My recent tour of the Seventh Armored Brigade, courtesy of the Friends of the Israeli Defense Forces, began with a lecture about the history of the Tank Corps. The rusting hulks of old armored trucks that line the road to Jerusalem are a memorial to Israel's first armored column, ancient vehicles protected by a "sandwich" of iron plates and plywood that broke the Arab siege of Jerusalem and brought food, water and ammunition to a beleaguered population. Thus was born the Seventh Brigade.

The public relations officer standing before us is a young woman of eighteen or nineteen. She describes the famous tank battles of the Mitla Pass, in Sinai, the Vale of Tears on the Golan and countless others. In the nearby Friends of the I.D.F. "Moadon" (recreation room) she introduces us to three of her friends. At first glance they seem to be teenagers listening to the latest hit record and enjoying some well-earned time off. In fact these young women are tank instructors, assigned to make drivers and gunners, and eventually commanders, out of young boys. One thought keeps insinuating itself into my head: these girls are not much older than my own daughter. How would I react if my daughter had to serve for two years in the army on the front lines of a country continually at war? The implications are terribly disconcerting. In essence children are defending the state of Israel, and, by extension, the Jewish people around the world.

Every citizen's son and daughter is expected on the front lines. Young men and women may be called upon to give their blood for the preservation of the Jewish homeland. This sobering thought puts into perspective the relationship between Israel and the "Golah" (diaspora). We give our money; they give their blood. We sacrifice our standard of living; they sacrifice their sons and daughters.

Out in the field we visit a company just beginning their training. The young recruits are all from "Yeshivot Hesder," which means they are students in a unique program that allows them to alternate Yeshiva study with Army service until their tour of duty is completed. This process can take up to five years instead of the usual three years if served consecutively. I have the distinct honor of being escorted by the Brigade commander (age 27) and the brigade chaplain, who is a Lubavitch Rabbi with a long beard. He has been briefed that I am a volunteer chaplain in the United States Airforce, and we compare notes. He is extremely knowledgeable about tanks and he answers all my questions about armor-piercing capabilities and high tech protective shields with facility. I learn that he himself served as a tank commander before he began his studies as a rabbi.

The Merkava tank is reputed to be the best in the world because, as every "tankist" will tell you, it was designed around the soldier, to give him every possible protection. The only way to begin to understand what a tank is all about is to sit in one. When the brigade commander gestures to one of the company tanks, I climb up and slither down into the driver's seat. Visualize four men sitting practically on top of one another: commander, driver, gunner, and loader. There is no room to move. I am trapped inside a steel box, claustrophobia gnawing at the back of my head, trying to understand what it means to be traveling across rough terrain at 60 or 70 kilometers per hour. How can you keep from cracking your skull or smashing your ribs against the nearest steel plate? How does the driver keep his eye in the periscope while bouncing up and down? How do you locate the enemy? How do you get out after taking a direct hit when you can barely turn in your seat? How do you come out alive?

Until you sit in a tank, even when standing still, you don't understand what the reality of war is. It has nothing to do with the romance of a Hollywood movie; it is greasy and dirty, and sweaty. And your life and the life of your crew depends on every move you make. And if you come back alive you had better thank G-d, and thank your instructors, and thank your buddies whose skill and bravery brought you home.

Current American State Department thinking views the Golan Heights as an inconsequential piece of real estate in an age of long-range missiles. From a desk in Washington the few Square kilometers of the Golan seem an obvious offering to the belligerent Syrians. What could it really matter to the Israelis? But the view from the Golan is entirely different. Wars are still fought with conventional arms: tanks are still called upon to defend territory and to neutralize attacking armies. The only factor that will force the Syrians to pursue peace instead of war is the Seventh Armored Brigade, who can be at the entrance to Damascus within one hour's notice.

Furthermore, the highest point in the Golan is a ridge of mountains at the easternmost edge of the Plateu facing Syria. It is here that the Israelis have established a chain of sophisticated listening posts that enables them to counter an attack even before the terrorists have started their engines. On the western edge of the Golan Heights the old Syrian artillery emplacements can still be seen. From here they shelled the Upper Galilee with impunity, making the life of the kibbutzniks in the Huleh Valley a living hell, until they were driven off in the 1967 "six day war." No one in his right mind could conceive of allowing the Syrians to move back into those gun emplacements, the American State Department notwithstanding.

Tonight the young men and women of the Seventh Armored Brigade will spend a few quiet moments as guests of the Friends of the IDF in their base "Moadon" (recreation center). With their comrades in hundreds of IDF recreation centers all across Israel they enjoy a little corner of the world that reminds them of home and family. Good music, a tasty sandwich, a comfortable chair, the latest magazine. And then they will shoulder their machine guns, climb into their tanks and go off into the night on patrol. While the people of Tel Aviv sleep in peace, their sons and daughters are off protecting the peace. At the crack of dawn pious Jews in Jerusalem will pray to G-D for their safety. And if they fail to return, a mother will cry and a father will recite the Kaddish, and a contingent of soldiers will stand at attention at an open grave in the military cemetery; and the ultimate price will have been exacted for the preservation of the State of Israel.

Another Arab Pogrom at the Temple Mount
November, 1990

When the Palestinian Arabs gathered on the Temple Mount during the Succot holiday to stone Jewish worshippers at the Kotel (western wall), they were following in the tradition of their ancestors. During the British Mandate Jews were often attacked at the Kotel by Arabs at the behest of their religious leaders and with the tacit approval of the British authorities. Dozens of Jews were murdered by Arab mobs incited to violence from the mosques in a series of pogroms that finally ended with the declaration of Jewish statehood and its active defense, beginning in 1948.

Make no mistake about it: The Arab riot at the Temple Mount was another attempt to kill the Jewish infidels who have dared to usurp the Muslim presence in Jerusalem. A rock directed at a skull kills just as surely as a bullet; and projected onto the Kotel Plaza from some fifty feet above the area it attains the velocity of a catapulted missile.

It was only a miracle that no Jews were killed outright, a point repeated by several commentators. Actually they seemed disappointed that there were no Israeli casualties, and they pointed to the lack of Jewish dead as proof of the fact that no Arab malice was intended: Just a few thousand Arab youths out for a friendly demonstration.

By using the holy Temple Mount as an arena for anti-Jewish violence, the Muslim Waqf (religious authority) has desecrated its own holy place, to say nothing of the Jewish holy site. Therefore they have forfeited any right to jurisdiction in the area and should be called upon to return the keys to the Israeli authorities. The Israelis have already demonstrated their sensitivity for the concerns and sensibilities of all the religions represented in Jerusalem. Their record at the Church of the Holy Sepulchre, the Armenian Church of St. James and the Al Aksa and Dome of the Rock mosques on the Temple Mount is impeccable. No other governing authority would have gone to such lengths at the expense of their own people.

The Arab attempt to reignite the intifada and to redirect attention away from Iraq's annexation of Kuwait and link the withdrawal from Judea and Samaria has been encouraged by the recent U.S.-sponsored resolution at the U.N. In 42 years, we have not seen one U.N. resolution condemning the murder of hundreds of Israeli civilians by Arab terrorists from Iran, Iraq, Syria, Libya, Jordan and Egypt. Neither have we seen a U.N. resolution condemning Syria's massacre of its own citizens in Hama and of Christians in Lebanon, or Jordan's execution of Palestinians, or Iraq's gassing of the Kurds, or Nelson Mandela's A.N.C. killing of black Zulus in South Africa or China's murder of students in Tianenmen Square or Palestinian Arabs' murder of their own people or hundreds of other incidents of brutality perpetrated by the sanctimonious "united nations." Only the Israels are singled out for public censure.

In the face of it all, Israeli police are accused of using excessive force. I wonder how the New York City police would react if worshippers leaving St. Patrick's Cathedral on Fifth Avenue would be accosted by a stone-throwing mob 3000 strong. The answer has already been given during the Harlem and Watts riots of the 1960's. Police were issued shotguns in Los Angeles and told to use them if necessary to maintain law and order, to say nothing about defending lives from rioters. But as usual Israel is subjected to that shameful, omnipresent double standard.

To make matters worse, a parallel is drawn between the Iraqui occupation of Kuwait and the so-called Israeli "occupation of the west bank." How many times need we reiterate that Iraq attacked and conquered Kuwait; but Jordan with the aid and encouragement of the Arab states attacked and tried to conquer Israel in 1967. The liberation of the "west bank" was one result. Furthermore, Jordan forfeited all claims in the west bank after rejecting the U.S. partition plan in 1948 and declaring war on Israel. And keep in mind that the territory called

Palestine, encompassing both sides of the Jordan river, was originally intended by the League of Nations to be divided into two states: one for Palestinian Jews and one for Palestinian Arabs. Instead, Britain arbitrarily created a country called Jordan and established the Hashemite monarchy in Amman. Faced with the loss of their country, Palestinian Arabs then sought to displace the Palestinian Jews.

The United Nations at best ignores the historical facts and at worst distorts them. A United Nations that resolved to equate Zionism with racism has forfeited any claim to moral or political leadership; and any resolution emanating from its chambers concerning Israel is automatically null and void. And this new coalition of America and Arab states will ultimately crumble under the pressure of Muslim fundamentalism, Arab dictatorship and regional medieval thinking. Only Israel, the sole modern democracy in the Middle East, has enough in common with the United States to form any lasting alliance.

The St. John's Hospice Controversy: Whose City Is It Anyway?

In the year 1000 B.C.E. King David established his capital on the Ophel Ridge in the city of URU SALEM, better known to the world as Jerusalem. Three hundred years later King Hezekiah defended an expanded city that included the so-called "Western Hill," where the present Jewish and Armenian quarters are located. By the time King Herod came to power in 37 B.C.E. the city, according the maximalist theory advanced by Biblical archaeologists, included all of what is encompassed in today's "old city" and much more.

Jerusalem was a Jewish city, the capital of a Jewish state. There was no Muslim, or Christian or Armenian quarter, because these people were several hundred years away from making their debut on the stage of world history. There was no Church of the Holy Sepulchre; it would be located at its present spot by Constantine's Roman mother, Queen Helena, in 326 C.E. And the cornerstone of the modern church would not be placed until the advent of the Crusaders in 1099.

There was no Dome of the Rock Mosque on the Temple Mount. It would be built by Caliph Abd-El-Malik, some 50 years after the Muslim conquest in 638 C.E.

It was the Romans who tried to eradicate Jerusalem. They burned the city and the holy temple after two bloody but unsuccessful Jewish revolts against their occupation. In 135 C.E. Hadrian demolished the city, exiled the Jews, and established a "Judenrein" Roman town called Colonia Aelia Capitolina. Jews were banned from living in the city until the fifth century. Their homes and property were appropriated first by Roman pagans and then by the early Christians, under Byzantine rule.

It was the Romans who rebuilt the city into four quarters,

defined by two intersecting avenues: the Cardo Maximus running roughly from to-day's Zion Gate to the Damascus Gate
through the Arab Souk; and the Decumanus starting at the
Jaffa Gate and ending at the Temple Mount (which was used as
a garbage dump until the Muslim period).

The Muslims allowed some Jews to return, and for the first
time, three religions lived in the city.

Both the Jews and the Muslims were slaughtered by the
Christian Crusaders in 1099, but they returned after Salah-el-
Din (an Armenian Muslim from Kurdistan) defeated the Chris-
tians in 1187.

When Salah-el-Din allowed the Jews to return they began
settling near the Western Wall, to-day's Jewish quarter. The
Armenians only consolidated their quarter in the 17th century
around the church of St. James over the vehement objections
of the Greek Orthodox community. The Christians were reduced to living in the vicinity of the Church of the Holy
Sepulchre, the modern Christian Quarter. The conquering
Muslims spread around the city, but were eventually concen-
trated in the northeast sector, and by the dawn of the 20th
century, the various major denomination occupied their present quarters.

In 1967, the Israeli army repelled an attack by King Hussein
and the Jordanians, and liberated the entire city of Jerusalem.
Not since the last days of the Bar-Kochba revolt in 135 C.E. had
the capital city of the Jewish people been in Jewish hands.

Not wishing to disturb the western democracies, and feeling
a sensitivity for the religious needs of the various foreign sects,
Israel maintained the status-quo. This status-quo was established by and inherited from the occupying powers of almost
2,000 years who had one thing in common: the attempted
reduction or elimination of the Jewish population in Jerusalem.
Had the Israeli army and government acted immediately to
"rebuild" the entire old city to better reflect its Jewish character;
and had it relocated several of the foreign religious monuments
built over the rubble and ashes of Jewish holy sites, the status-
quo would have been drastically changed. A hue and cry would
have gone up from the world from the same governments who

were strangely silent when Jewish synagogues were dyna-
mited, or used as stables and latrines, and when Jews were
banned from praying at the Western Wall. But the noise would
have dissipated, as the media grew tired of the same old story.

And then no one would have uttered a word when Jews
moved into any neighbourhood in their city.

The St. John's Hospice has a cross over its doorway. The first
cross wasn't officially seen in Jerusalem until the Byzantines
came to rule. (That is, the first cross not used as an instrument
of Roman execution.) The hospice was built on Jewish property
without the consent of the original owners, who had probably
been displaced and/or murdered by Christian conquerors.

Even so, in an effort to be scrupulously fair, the Israeli
government leased the property from the present owner. What
other people would pay to retrieve their own property, in their
own country?

Jerusalem has been the capital of the Jewish State for almost
3000 years. No one will dictate to Jews where they may not live
in their own capital city. And no one should accuse us of
religious insensitivity. We have bent over backwards at our own
expense to safeguard access to all the religious monuments in
the city. How disappointing that even some of our own Jewish
organizations have forgotten this, and are so quick to parrot
the U.S. State Department with declarations of "insensitive
and provocative."

If the second week of April is considered an "insensitive"
time to call the moving vans, then when is a good time? The
fact remains that the Christians and Muslims in Jerusalem
refuse to acknowledge that the city is the capital of the Jewish
State; and the rest of the world, the western democracies and
the Vatican included, encourage this obstinacy by joining in
this stubborn refusal and by threatening to reduce foreign aid
as a gesture of appeasement to the Arab bloc.

The Israelis are not about to repay Christian and Muslim
barbarism by ejecting them from the city. But Jews can and
should insist on their right to live anywhere they choose in
their own city in accordance with accepted legal procedures

that govern the lease and sale of property. Peaceful coexistence will come only when this principle is accepted by all, and when the world officially recognizes Jerusalem as the indivisible capital of the State of Israel.

Congressional Record:
A Palestinian State Called Jordan

Proceedings and Debates of the 102d Congress, First Session

Washington, Tuesday, April 23, 1991, Vol.137, No. 60—House of Representatives:

RABBI BARRY KONOVITCH'S ARTICLE

HON. ILEANA ROS-LEHTINEN
OF FLORIDA
IN THE HOUSE OF REPRESENTATIVES
Tuesday, April 23, 1991

Ms. ROS-LEHTINEN, Mr. Speaker, an interesting article appeared in the Miami Herald, El Nuevo Herald, and the Miami Jewish Tribune and I would like to bring it to the attention of my colleagues. It was written by Rabbi Barry Konovitch and he reminds us of the importance of the establishing peace in the Middle East. Rabbi Konovitch states that "it is the time to settle the Palestinian issue and remove it as a stumbling block to peace."

I am hereby reprinting it in the CONGRESSIONAL RECORD:

I thank and commend Rabbi Konovitch for his efforts for reminding the south Florida community of the importance in supporting Israel. Rabbi Konovitch has done a remarkable job by defining that the war for Israel continues.

The battle of the Scud missiles may be over, but for Israel the war continues. The Arab states persist in their belligerent policy of "non-recognition and non-discussion," using the issue of the Palestinians as an excuse for their refusal to recognize the right of the Jewish people to their own state in their national homeland, an inalienable right for all nations in the world.

26

It is time to settle the Palestinian issue and remove it as a stumbling block to peace.

The term Palestine was first used to describe the Jewish homeland by the Romans who attempted to destroy the national connection between Jews and their state of Judea. Not only did they erase Judea from the map by substituting the name of the coastal "sea people," the Philistines (mortal enemies of the Israelites), but they even had the audacity to erase the name of Jerusalem, substituting Aelia Capitolina after the emperor Aelius Adrianus and the god of Rome.

When the British, under Lord Allenby, defeated the Ottoman Turks in World War One, they were mandated by the League of Nations to administer Palestine, which included the territory on both sides of the Jordan (what is today Israel and Jordan).

Britain issued the Balfour Declaration looking with favor on the creation of the modern Jewish State within the Palestine mandate, while at the same time expecting to create a parallel Arab state. This would satisfy the national aspirations of the Palestinian Jews and Arabs who both lived in the area. In 1921, the British arbitrarily divided Palestine in half, giving the Trans-Jordan sector to the Arabs and establishing Abdullah, son of Sherif Hussein of the Hedjaz, as King. His brother Feisal had already been installed as King of Syria, only to be opposed by the French authorities of the Syrian mandate. The British then placed him on the throne of Iraq. Thus did the British pay their debts to the Hashemites, by reducing Palestine to the area west of the Jordan river. Here the British proposed to divide the remaining mandate territory once again between the Jewish Palestinians and the Arab Palestinians. The Jews had little choice but to accept any agreement that would promote the establishment of the State of Israel. However, the Arabs refused to accept any Jewish presence in the Middle East and went to war in 1948.

The Palestinians became an issue only some twenty years later when Israel liberated the West Bank after being attacked by a combined force of Arab states that included King Hussein of Jordan. For 20 years the Arabs had refused to make peace and continued to attempt to destroy the Jewish State, while

there was no "Palestinian problem"; Jordan ruled the West
Bank. Obviously the reason for Arab intransigence had nothing
to do with the Palestinians. From day one the Arabs refused to
accept the existence of a Jewish State, and that remains the
main obstacle to peace in the Middle East.

The conclusion of the Persian Gulf War presents an opportunity for peace. It has underscored the fact that Arab hatred
for Jews is almost matched by Arab hatred for Arabs, witness
the brutality of the Iraqi occupation of Kuwait and the continued brutalizing of the West Bank Palestinian Arabs by the PLO
under the guise of the Intifada. This underlines a primary
requirement for peace: a secure State of Israel, whose borders
must be accepted by the Arab States but guaranteed by the
world community because monarchic and dictatorial Arab re-
gimes are subject to constant revolutions and counterrevolu-
tions.

The State of Israel, where the Jewish Palestinians live, includes the area west of the Jordan. The State of Jordan where
the Arab Palestinians live, comprising 70% of the population,
includes the area east of the Jordan. There is no need to create
a second Palestinian Arab state, as there is no need to create a
second Palestinian Jewish state. Arabs living in Israel, either in
the West Bank or the Galilee, have several choices: become
citizens of Jordan, or citizens of Israel, or establish local civil
autonomy with informal connections to Jordan and/or Israel. If
Arabs feel a need to live in a formal Palestinian state, then they
may move to Jordan, as Jews in Arab lands who felt a need to
live in a Jewish State have moved to Israel. Whichever option is
chosen there is only one proviso: live in peace.

Letter from Yitzhak Shamir
Tel Aviv, 23 August, 1992

Rabbi Barry J. Konovitch
2045 N.E. 186th Drive
No. Miami Beach, FL 33179

Dear Rabbi Konovitch,

I thank you for your heartfelt wishes.

I look back with satisfaction upon those active terms of government under my leadership, and note the many critical achievements which we attained, despite the many difficulties with which we were faced.

From all aspects, we have firmly placed the State of Israel in a strong position.

I am, however, concerned by the fact that as a result of the last elections, those policies which I have implemented will not continue and our achievements may deteriorate. I hope that the Jewish people in Israel and in the Diaspora will prevent dangerous mistakes in the future and will avert political misdirection.

Sincerely,

Yitzhak Shamir

The Nazis of "New" Germany

Almost 50 years later the sadistic German welcome, "Arbeit Macht Frei," is clearly etched in the main gate. It was here in Dachau, a quiet town on the outskirts of Munich, that the Nazis began their program to rid Germany of the "undesirables." German history in these last six decades plays like a Wagnerian opera: from the Gotterdämmerung to the rise of the Phoenix. But German politics exhibits a déja vu that is beginning to frighten and threaten. Neo-Nazis attack refugees; the German government concludes a deal to deport thousands of gypsies to Romania; youths with shaved heads speak of the need to cleanse Germany of all foreign elements; Adolph Hitler is quoted as sage and prophet and admired by the youngest generation as a hero.

We remember clearly that what started with the elimination of the gypsies ended with the murder of the Jews, and what began in Germany quickly spread across Europe. In 1942 Romania had already murdered 300,000 Jews. The government realized it could sell the remaining Jews. During the communist regime again the Jews were for sale, this time to Israel. Nothing seems to ever change.

Commentators are quick to point out the differences between Germany then and now. The commentators usually have Protestant sounding names, with faces to match and a family history that records no missing members in Dachau. Those of us who have seen the tattooed numbers and heard the eyewitness accounts of the survivors are not so quick to dismiss the stoning of a foreigners' hostel in North Germany as an aberration. This dangerous behavior is the rule in Germanic society, not the exception. The urge to "final solutions" seems part of German blood, and barbarism comes naturally to those weaned on the Valküre's milk. And all Germans are responsible for the renaissance of nazism as they were all responsible for the concentration camps.

The problem with this line of thinking is that those individuals who actually committed the crimes are now hidden behind "all of Germany." If all Germans are responsible then we do not hold individuals accountable. How do we bring a whole country to trial; how do we punish a whole country?

In fact it was and still is individuals who are responsible. Some one person with a name and a face fired the machine guns at the killing fields. Someone kicked the stool out from under the gallows. Someone dashed the infant against the wall. Someone poured the Zyklon Z into the gas chamber. And someone gave each order for torture and death.

The barbed wire at Dachau is still in place, albeit rusted, as are the watchtowers, and the crematoriums. Large groups of youngsters stand silently as their teachers quietly recount the horrors of the past. Will they now speak up as Nazism reappears in modern Germany; or will their silence serve to encourage the monster? And what is the difference between the man who raised the pistol and the man who raised no protest? Silence can be as deafening as a gunshot, and guilt comes in an active and passive form.

At Dachau the main gate still locks shut. On whom this time?

To Be or Not to Be

When the Japanese bombed Pearl Harbor, declaring war against the United States, the American high command could not understand what happened. How could the Japanese have dared challenge the power of the mightiest nation on earth? What made them think that the United States could be defeated?

After the war, the question was put to the Japanese general staff. The answer was as follows: "We saw training films of American recruits practicing with broom-sticks instead of guns. We noticed that you never bothered to fortify your Pacific Island bases. And we saw your Senate pass a concription act by only one vote and after much negative debate and hesitation."

The Japanese concluded that America was indecisive, that Americans were unable or unwilling to defend themselves, that Americans would never go to war, that America could not agree on a plan of action.

Our inability to make decisions was perceived by the enemy as weakness; and Japan attacked on the basis of their analysis of our weakness. The result was a World War that took millions of lives.

Whenever we cannot or will not make decisions, we are perceived as weak and disorganized. We invite disaster.

Making decisions is never easy.

Occasionally we make a mistake and we have to pay for it. But we can always correct a mistake.

However, nothing is worse than no decision. A decision implies movement, progress and dynamism. Indecision implies stasis, stagnation and paralysis.

In 1948 David Ben Gurion had to make a decision. Should he declare the independent State of Israel or should he wait for a more opportune time? Should he wait for support and recognition from the world's democracies or should the Jewish people put their trust in G-d and in their own abilities? Ben-Gurion decided that if he hesitated, the State of Israel would never be born. It was his decisive, unequivocal action that brought us independence after 2,000 years of exile. It is for this reason that Ben Gurion will forever be remembered as a great leader. The price of leadership is decision, and the price of progress is positive action.

In 1973 Golda Meir had to make a decision. Should she call up the reserves and prepare for war with Egypt, or should she wait for Henry Kissinger and the vagaries of American foreign policy? Should she order a pre-emptive strike against Cairo to defend Israel, or should she wait for Egypt to make the first move? She hesitated, afraid to make a decision. The result was the first time in modern history that Israel seemed on the verge of defeat. The Bar-Lev line was overrun; the Egyptians swarmed across the Suez Canal, and the Israelis retreated.

The war ended in victory, but it was a bitter one. Israel has not been the same since. For many years paralysis and self-recrimination seized the country. And Golda Meir never recovered. She went to her grave realizing that her indecision had almost destroyed the country.

Each of us, in our business and personal lives, will be called upon to make crucial decisions. Let us not hesitate; let us not be fearful. If our decision is based on intelligence, insight, balance and truth then we shall make the right decision. And if occasionally circumstances prove us wrong, then so be it. We will do better the next time. None of us is perfect and we can only proceed to the best of our abilities.

But let us have the courage to make a decision.

A decision, any decision, is still better than no decision.

The Art of Communication and the "United Nonsense"

During our travels in Israel last summer we spent a good deal of time listening to the comments of our bus driver. Often the discussion would turn to Israeli politics on the international scene, and he would take great pleasure in referring to that building in Manhattan where the representatives of the world's nations gather, as "the United Nonsense." I often think of the United Nations as a "Tower of Babel" where many people talk, but no one is really listening; where people speak *at* one another instead of *to* each other. The *New York Times* recently wrote: "The United Nations is marking 40 years; it has aged, but not matured."

I would not be so charitable. The U.N. has regressed, especially when it comes to dealing with our State of Israel. Any organization that labels "Zionism as racism" does not merit our serious attention, much less our financial support. As Americans we reject the ongoing attempt to subvert the only true democracy in the Middle East, the only reliable and steadfast ally of the United States.

Perhaps the only encouraging thought is that the nations of the world are still talking. Even in a world plagued by war and terrorism, there are still more words exchanged than bullets. Where there is discussion there is still hope for improvement.

The same principle operates in our personal lives. The virtual epidemic of child abuse and wife beating evident in American society is a direct result of the inability to communicate in a mature manner.

Our tradition emphasizes this concept and goes one step forward: not only is communication essential, but *how* we communicate is equally important. Jewish literature is filled with admonitions to treat the people around us with verbal sensitivity. What comes out of our months can never be taken back, and the damage caused by a wrong word can be more devastating than a weapon.

Furthermore, communication involves two parties: we generally are not interested in talking to ourselves. It is equally important to be a good listener as a good talker. If everyone is talking, but no one is listening, then again there is no real communication. If the finest words are "going in one ear and out the other" then the attempt at meaningful dialogue is doomed.

I have noted that often it is more difficult to be a good listener than a good talker, because it involves closing your mouth once in a while. And closing our mouths is something we are reluctant to do.

Each day we recite a beautiful prayer at the end of the Amidah: "Lord prevent my tongue from speaking evil and my lips from speaking guile."

It is evil to wound the feelings of our fellow men and it is inexcusable not to speak to each other as "menschen."

Our ability and willingness to communicate as "menschen" determines our claim to the title of "civilized people."

That Was a Seder

In April of 1964 I only celebrated one Seder instead of the customary two.

Before you begin to wonder what strange ideas obsessed Rabbi Konovitch in the spring of '64 let me ease your mind. I was a resident of Jerusalem at the time and although it turned out to be a temporary residence, Rabbinic law dictated that I adopt the law of the land. After all, anyone who spends a length of time in Israel stands a good chance of establishing permanent roots in the holy soil.

Actually I had it on good authority that any young man who spends a length of time in Israel cannot help but be intoxicated by the beauty of the land. And since Israeli beauty comes in many shapes and sizes it was a foregone conclusion that a "permanent arrangement" would be forthcoming. And so it was that I spent the most fascinating Seder of my life in a place called Tel-Nof, not far from the city of Rechovot.

Tel Nof is one of the major air force bases in the country and the latest Israeli acquisitions are based here. A visitor would hardly know that he was inside an airforce base because there are no planes to be seen. In a country situated so close to enemy eyes, camouflage is an indispensable part of airforce security.

Only the hangars were visible and it was in one of these huge buildings that the seder was to be held. Imagine a seder held in an airplane hangar, with the walls decorated by camouflage netting, just a few short air-minutes away from the scene of the very first seder in Jewish history.

A few thousand men and women, together with all the Jewish military attachés in the Middle East who could manage to beg, borrow or steal a lift into Tel Nof, were present for the great occasion.

As a personal guest of Rabbi Shlomo Goren, Chief Chaplain

of the Israeli armed forces, I was privileged to be in great company. Surrounding me were the gallant men who made Israel what it is today. It was difficult to distinguish the officers from the men and soon everyone seemed to be on first name basis.

The kiddush heralded the beginning of the Seder, and each commander went down the aisle with his own bottle, filling the glasses of each of his men. The shouts of Le'Chaim reverberated through the hangar as each officer joined his men in the traditional toast.

When the time came to recite Avadim Hayinu, Rabbi Goren rose in his seat and led the recounting of our ancient relationship to Egypt. The words literally came to life. Those men weren't reciting the history of yesteryear. It was apparent that they were speaking about yesterday, and today and the days that would follow. It was safe to assume that the plagues suffered by the ancient Egyptians would be nothing compared to the damage that would be inflicted by these modern Hebrew stalwarts. History was repeating itself. The conflict with the Pharaoh was continuing. But no one had to turn to the end of the Haggadah to predict the final outcome.

The Seder lasted far into the night, and the memories of that occasion will last forever. When peace finally comes to the land of Israel a new page will be written into the Haggadah. It will tell of those glorious young men and women of Israel who refused to submit to a modern Pharaoh. And who, with the help of the Lord, brought about a miracle that shall never be forgotten.

Who Is a Jew: Another Opinion

The question of "Who is a Jew" as it relates to the "Law of Return" presents a complicated and often confusing issue. On the one hand it is is an internal Israeli matter. One for the sovereign State of Israel through its Parliament to define. Israel has its legal standards of citizenship as does the United States; and no one may demand the lowering of those standards, certainly not those who have no intention of ever petitioning for citizenship. On the other hand the Law of Return theoretically affects the entire Jewish world through the hoped-for movement of "aliyah," the expected dissolution of the Diaspora in favor of settlement in our historical homeland.

Further confusion lies in the failure to differentiate between the definition of the Israeli government for purposes of citizenship and the definition of the Chief Rabbinate for purposes of Halacha (Jewish Law).

As the Law of Return is presently formulated, any convert to Judaism is automatically entitled to Israeli citizenship, a purely secular status. But if such a convert wishes to marry then he would fall under the juridisction of the Israeli rabbinical authorities who would then be obligated to apply a religious-legal definition (halachic). A non-Orthodox conversion would not be acceptable for purposes of marriage. But it would not affect citizenship, which does not fall within the juridisction of the rabbinate. This is the way the law of return has been understood and applied; and I believe this is the way it should remain.

But even if the Law of Return were to be amended it would have no effect on the Jews of America who have no interest in moving to Israel. Anyone converted in America by any rabbi is still considered Jewish in their respective communities. It is quite misleading to maintain that a modification in the Law of Return to accept only those converted by the Orthodox rabbinate would automatically invalidate the "Jewishness of hundreds of American converts." And if any of these non-Orthodox converts ever wish to emigrate to Israel, at the very "worst" they would be "reconverted" by the Israeli rabbinate, a process that is accessible to anyone. The truth of the matter is that various communal and religious figures in American Jewish life wish to dictate religious policy to Israel by subtle and not so subtle monetary threats. We cannot tolerate these arrogant threats to the welfare of the people and the State of Israel. Israel has given us much more that we can ever hope to give her in return. It is our privilege, nay our holy obligation to support the State.

And if we wish to take part in her political process then all we have to do is buy a one way ticket on EL-AL airlines, destination Ben-Gurion Airport. It seems preposterous for Jews living in Brooklyn or Miami beach to dictate anything to the citizens of Israel, and interfere in their internal affairs.

The Law of Return recognizes the inalienable right of every Jew to return to his homeland and be granted automatic citizenship. For more than three thousand years, we had no problem defining who was a Jew: a person born of a Jewish mother or converted in accordance with established rabbinic procedures (halacha). The attempt to tamper with these traditional procedures and definitions constitutes an attempt to dilute the Jewish people. It is a capitulation to the pressures of a Jewish philantrophic establishment riddled by assimilation and unable or unwilling to maintain the standards of Jewish life.

Unfortunately, the matter of "Mi-hu-Yehudi" (Who is a Jew) has been thrown into the Israeli political arena. It needs to be removed from the Knesset along with all matters of religious law (halacha) and considered only in the arena of the Rabbinical Court and the Chief Rabbinate. The definition of "Jewishness" is much too important and sacred an issue to be used as a political football.

Furthermore, leaders on both sides of the Atlantic and on both ends of the religious spectrum do not serve the interests of the Jewish people by fomenting division, recriminations and hysteria. We have enough problems surviving the "slings and arrows" of a hostile world without weakening ourselves from within.

What is needed is the convening of an international rabbinical council representing the entire Jewish world, in order to adopt a universally acceptable definition of "Who is a Jew." Not for the sake of the State of Israel which is entitled to determine its own definitions of statehood, but for the sake of a unified and indivisible Jewish people. We cannot afford to fragment ourselves into hostile camps and opposing forces. We do not deserve an independent state if we do not have the intelligence, pride and religious commitment to unite with all Jewish people and with the State of Israel in a permanent expression of solidarity.

This definition of jewishness should be based on the "Jewish Constitution," the Torah of Israel, the immutable law that has preserved us intact for three millennia. Likewise the State of Israel must be a "Jewish State," not merely a "State of Jews." And the process of raising the standard of Jewish life in Israel must be one of education, and not coercion or even legislation. We no longer live in a theocratic state governed by the Sanhedrin in the shadow of the holy Temple. Instead, Israel presents itself as a democracy, and as such must be open to the mandates of its people no matter what their religious or political viewpoint. In such circumstances, the Rabbinate of Israel is called upon to educate the people, not coerce them; not legislatively and certainly not physically. No one ever became more religious from a rock aimed at his head. The Rabbinate must recapture the respect of the people by depoliticizing religion. And it must influence the people by reaching out to them with enlightenment, compassion, love, tolerance and understanding. And it must educate the people in Israel as well as Jewish people around the world to understand the beauty and relevance of our tradition, and the necessity of the concept of "am echad" (one people).

I trust that all this will not be labeled mere "messianic musings"—because the future of the people of Israel depends on it. We have always been able to deal with external pressures; it has always been internal divisiveness that defeats us. Let us, therefore, stand together; with faith in G-d, with respect for one another, and with hope for the future.

Homestead Air Force Base Presentation fosters ties with Israeli air force

Maj. Margaret Stanek
31st Public Affairs Division

With the acceptance of two aerial photos depicting an F-15 flying over the temple site in Jerusalem, Homestead AFB symbolically sealed a loop in a chain of friendship and shared purpose linking this stateside base with its counterpart in the Negev desert in Israel.

Col. Charles Magsig, deputy commander for operations, and Col. Donald Sullenberger, 31st Combat Support Group commander, accepted the two framed and dedicated F-15 aerial photos from Rabbi Barry Konovitch during a staff meeting at wing headquarters this week.

According to the rabbi, the exchange was a return gesture of camaraderie and mission sent to the base by Nevatim Air Base in Israel, demonstrating the "bonds of respect, love and mutual friendship that Israel and America share."

Rabbi Konovitch, the rabbi for Homestead AFB personnel who is also affiliated with the Temple Beth Shmuel in Miami, was personally responsible for the idea of introducing the two different air bases to each other. Invited by the Israeli government to dedicate land designated for future forest development in Israel, Rabbi Konovitch approached the 31st Tactical Fighter Wing's command section with the idea of sending a token of their respect and good wishes to their Israeli counterparts. Two wing patches and letters from Col. Hale Burr, 31st TFW commander, and Colonel Sullenberger were carried by the rabbi to Nevatim Air Base, in Israel's southern desert. In return, the commanders of the Israeli base sent back their best wishes and the F-15 photos.

Since F-15s are generally a rarity on an F-16 base, the rabbi was asked the significance of the photos.

"The F-15, an American-manufactured fighter, represents (our) determination to insure peace in the world," the rabbi explained. The image of the F-15 over Jerusalem's temple mount—one of the holiest areas in the world—strongly reinforces this theme, the rabbi said.

"The picture is definitely a special tribute," Rabbi Konovitch said. "There are very few of them around, and they're not given out lightly."

Letter from Col. Benjamin Zinker, I.D.F.

Colonel H. Hale Burr Jr, USAF
Commander.
31st. Tactical Fighter Wing (TAC).
Homestead Air Force Base.
U.S.A.

Dear Colonel Burr,

Thank you for your greetings and best wishes sent to us by the 31st Tactical Fighter Wing from sunny Florida. They were warmly received.

I would like to extend our friendship, inviting you to see our sunny Ramon Air Base, which I'm sure would be an interesting and pleasurable visit.

Let's continue to try and make peace a reality.

Sincerely,

Benjamin Zinker—Col.
Base Commander

Letter from Col. Hale Burr, USAF

Department of the Air Force
Headquarters 31st Tactical Fighter Wing (TAC)
Homestead Air Force Base FL 33039-5000

Colonel Benjamin Zinker
Commandant
Ramon Air Base, Israel

Dear Colonel Zinker

It is my pleasure to send greetings and best wishes to you from the 31st Tactical Fighter Wing (Tactical Air Command) Homestead Air Force Base, Florida, via Rabbi Barry Konovitch, our Jewish Chaplain.

In this time of testing, when the principles of democracy are under atack around the world, Israel and America join in the defense of free people everywhere.

May peace come in our time.

Sincerely

H. Hale Burr, Jr.,
Colonel, USAF
Commander

Lost in the Shuk

In the halcyon days before the intifada when Arab residents of Jerusalem carried loaves of bread instead of AK-47s and Tel-Avivians shopped in the *shuk* without fear of attack, we lived for a summer in the *rova*, the newly rebuilt Jewish quarter. It was 1978 and we were in the holy city to begin an archaeological excavation of the city of David on the Ophel ridge just south of the present "old city" walls. The work was exciting but extremely hard and enervating in the hot summer sun and the constant dust. We looked forward to Shabbat when we could rise well after the daily 4:30 AM work call, and leisurely stroll to the Yemenite minyan at the Yochanan ben Zakkai synagogue. My son Jonathan was made an honorary Yemenite after he joined the youngsters in their distinctive chant of Yimloch as the Torah was returned to the ark. We felt comfortable and safe. We were at home in our city, in our homeland.

After the obligatory afternoon nap we would call on our good friend Kara'in who invariably sat in the shade cast by his shop wall, a stone's throw from the Lion's Gate. The route took us from the Jewish quarter, through the various Arab markets, known collectively as the *shuk*, down the Via Dolorosa and into the Christian quarter. Kara'in was a resident of Silwan and often invited us to sit on his terrace in late afternoon shielded from the sun by his grape arbor, to admire the view as shadows outlined ancient burial caverns across the valley. It was much the same view accorded to King David from his palace window. Three thousand years had passed but the scenery had scarcely changed.

On this particular Shabbat we took leave of Kara'in on the Lion's Gate Road and Jonathan elected to run ahead of me as I lingered for an extended goodbye. I was unconcerned as Jonathan knew his way around the old city like a native and would often go shopping for us by himself in the neighborhood.

Many of the shop-keepers, Jew and Arab, knew him by name. When I returned to our apartment, I realized that he had not returned. My concern mounted until it turned to panic. Jonathan was lost in the *shuk*. What could have happened to him? Had he been kidnapped or worse?

I begin to retrace my route, running as fast as I could go in the crowded narrow alleys, knocking over people in my way. Guilt and self-blame converged to drive me even faster and prompt a questioning of my sanity. How could I allow a child to go alone in an environment that could easily degenerate into one of hostility and even danger. Each shopkeeper and merchant became a potential threat as I swept the area, calling my son's name and engaging each set of Arab eyes with accusation.

As I turned the corner out of the covered market and started down the Via Dolorosa I heard his voice: "Abba!" There he was sitting with an Arab shopkeeper, drinking a Coca-cola. Out of breath I couldn't even ask for an explanation. The shopkeeper had noticed him crying, sat him down with a drink and assured him that his father would find him shortly, all in perfect English.

We were welcomed home by the police who, at the request of my wife, were just about to start a search. After a short rest and a promise to stay close from now on, we were on our way to *Shalosh Seudot*, (the traditional third meal of Shabbat) at the synagogue of the Ramban, selected not only for its proximity but for its tasty fare.

I often think back to those relatively peaceful days in Jerusalem when Arabs and Jews respected each other and still believed that it might be possible to live in peace together in the same city; and when a little Jewish boy could feel safe and at home in the alleys of the *shuk*; and when a Jewish father could feel eternally grateful to a Christian Arab for exhibiting that modicum of humanity that often serves as the bridge over troubled waters.

PART II
AMERICA AT WAR

Peace in Vietnam?

On February 3rd, precisely at 7:00 P.M., peace officially came to Vietnam. Peace on paper, that is. It will be quite a while before the last shot is fired. The longest, most destructive war in American history will make its effects felt for a long time to come. No other war in our entire history has had such a devastating effect upon the fabric of our own society. How ironic that a war taking place halfway around the world had such a horrible effect on the American people. Not one bomb fell on United States territory. Not one drop of blood was absorbed into American soil. Not one building was damaged; not one blade of grass disturbed. And yet we have been severely crippled. It will take years to repair the extensive moral and spiritual damage done to the American soul.

I can vaguely remember VJ-Day in New York City. Sometime in the late evening the word had arrived that the great war was at an end. People streamed into the streets in their nightgowns and pyjamas, dancing and singing for joy. I have never seen such a spontaneous outpouring of happiness and relief in America since.

That Saturday evening I listened hard for such a celebration. But it just didn't happen. No noise, no singing, no dancing, no joy, no celebration. Just business as usual.

Maybe no one really believed that the war was at an end. Maybe no one believed the T.V. newscasts and the newspaper headlines. And do you blame them? Think of all the times in the past several years that the American people have been cruelly fooled by the headlines. "Peace negotiations. Peace around the corner. Troops to come home." How many times can you play with the heartstrings of the American people, before they turn away in disgust. How many times can the government present fantasy as fact before the people lose their

49

entire faith in the system. Perhaps no one really believes that the war has really come to an end.

Or perhaps no one really cares. Many of us don't care because we choose to block the war out of our minds. The way we might block out a painful experience. We cannot face the situation. It has become too traumatic for us to consider. We have relegated it to limbo. It doesn't exist for us.

Once we could vividly remember the countless Vietnamese hamlets obliterated by mass bombing. We no longer wish to be reminded. Once we could remember the Vietnamese civilians running down the road afire from napalm bombardment. We choose not to be reminded. Once we could remember Mylai, and innocent victims of the war. Once we could remember the young men who would never come home. Once we could remember the tearful families. Once we could remember the sheer idiocy of this war. But we choose to forget.

But it is good for us to dredge up the bits and pieces of the war and take a good, hard look at them. To firmly and indelibly etch it into our memories so that we do not ever forget. So that hopefully we will never repeat such a disastrous mistake.

America has lost the first major conflict of her history. Oh, our governmental experts would vehemently deny my conclusion. They would point to the truce as a victory for the United States forces. But Hanoi is claiming the same thing.

The truth is that all sides are the losers. The casualties have been innumerable. Not just in terms of flesh and blood, but in terms of the spirit.

As we look back on the history of the last few decades, can anyone find a good reason for embarking on such a path in the first place? Can anyone in America remember why it was decreed that American men should end their young lives in a jungle several thousand miles from home? Can anyone in America remember why it was important to turn a whole country into one big bombed out crater? Can anyone in America remember why we took it upon ourselves to defend a country by destroying it? Yes, that's what I said. Defend a country by destroying it.

And on the home front we suffered no physical damage. But would anyone dare to say that we have not suffered any casualties? The greatest casualty of the war has been America. America, the land that was to be an example of righteous conduct to all the nations; a land governed by ethics and morality; government beyond reproach. I don't know whether to laugh or to cry. It will be years before the American people even begin to trust their own government again.

There were bombs dropped on America. They were dropped by the people who equated opposition to the war with opposition to America. Patriotism had to be expressed with a bullet or else it wasn't worth anything.

America: love it or leave it. Can you still remember that horrible expression of what has passed for patriotism?

Peace with honor. Do you remember that? We still hear about it. Peace with honor. Honor? What is honor? Where is honor in an episode that every responsible American would like to forget? Where is honor in dead bodies and a ravaged countryside? What honor! Peace with shame should be our statement. At least shame would indicate that we admit our terrible mistake. Shame would allow us to take the first step to heal our deep spiritual wounds. An insistence on honor would only serve to prolong our sickness.

It is time to acknowledge our mistakes, to accept our share of the guilt. The president should declare a national day of mourning and penitence. A Yom Kippur of sorts. Perhaps G-d and the world might see fit to forgive us. Perhaps the people of the world could find it in their hearts to excuse us. In a few years. A few decades.

Several weeks ago, I watched the special service in Key Biscayne in honor of the war's end. With the President in attendance, the pastor praised him for his fine efforts and prayed for his welfare. We all pray for America, and for its leaders. The Lord only knows how the last four administrations of America were in dire need of divine guidance. No one administration can be made to shoulder the full blame. All are to blame. The American people are to blame. Especially those who proudly displayed those confounded signs, America: love it or leave it.

We look forward to a leader who will have the courage to realize our mistake. A leader who will be able to pick up the pieces and make us spiritually whole once again. A leader who will be able to bring back a whole generation of alienated young; to convince them that America can really be all that it has been cracked up to be.

During that service in Key Biscayne, the pastor asked everyone present to rise and to join in the singing of "America the Beautiful." I was quite moved. It has been a long time since I could sing such a song with any positive feeling. It has been a long time since I was moved to any positive thoughts during the Star Spangled Banner. All that I could think about was the tremendous gap between the words of the song and the reality of America. For me, America the beautiful has only been a prophecy. What America could be. What America might be.

America the beautiful has been an epitaph for an America that died the day the first soldier set foot on Vietnamese soil. America the beautiful is a hope for a Techiat Hametim, a resurrection of the dead. A resurrection of hopes and dreams that have been dead for over a decade.

Last week I read of a strange incident concerning the returning prisoners. A marine who was believed to have been killed at Khe Sanh in 1968 and buried in a St. Louis cemetery, suddenly turned up alive as a prisoner of war. He will soon be reunited with his family.

If I were to sum up the war, if it is possible to sum up such a ghastly affair, I would sum it up in much the same manner.

America has been officially dead for over a decade. And now we are miraculously coming back to life. The nightmare is turning into a dream of hope for the future. War is giving way to peace. Death is giving way to life. The once dead soul of America is being resurrected.

May G-d teach us to learn from our mistakes. May he grant a lasting peace to our weary world. And as we wish each other Shabbat Shalom, let us pause to consider the words. Shalom. Peace. There is no greater blessing that the world could enjoy.

May he who establishes peace in the universe, bestow peace upon us, and upon the whole world, Amen.

Songmy Massacre

With the beginning of the 1970's, Americans are beginning to focus their attention on relatively new, and more "in vogue" problems. The most glaring and disastrous problem of the 60's, the Vietnam war, is fading into history. The uproar is dying down, the demonstrations are a thing of the past, and students will once again go about the serious business of acquiring an education without the spectre of a Vietnam battlefield lurking over their shoulders.

But the effects of this war are first beginning to be felt by our nation. For years to come we will have to nurse the sick American psyche back to health. No one can even begin to realize the brutalizing effect that the war has had on our very souls.

Recently the so-called incident at Songmy brought home to us just how terribly the Vietnam conflict has affected us, soldiers and civilian alike. The following letter was distributed by the Queens Interfaith Clergy Council and it should serve to drive the point home:

"What has happened to the conscience of American people when the massacre of men, women and children is called an 'incident'? How can we condone the destruction of a population and an agricultural nation on which we have dropped more bombs than fell on all of Europe in World War II? Where are our religious teachings when our young men shoot innocent men, women and children, call them 'gooks' and show no respect for the dignity and infinite worth of the human personality?

"Songmy shows the effect an unjust and senseless war can have on any man and any country. It is a dangerous condition when men are expected to equate support of the war with patriotism and conscientious protest is equated with failure to support our government. Our moral teachings are endangered and undermined when the quantitive standards of morality and progress are measured by body count.

"If Songmy can be ignored, then there is a serious moral breakdown in our country which will color our actions and will infect the main stream of our lives. We must with deep love and concern for our fellowmen pursue a path toward peace in Vietnam and heal the wounds of that unfortunate land.

"If the reports from the GI's themselves are even partially true—and they have not been denied—how can Americans remain silent without an overwhelming response of righteous indignation? We must frankly and with contrite spirit face the terrible fact of Songmy."

This now infamous incident at Songmy took place just a short while ago. A few voices of protest were heard, a few editorials of condemnation were read, and soon the whole affair was buried in the graveyard of history past. But make no mistake about it. Songmy is indelibly etched on the national conscience. It will be back time and again to haunt us to remind us that even the most civilized of people can fall victim to the savage impulses that abide within us all.

It is usually extremely difficult to keep our sense of morality intact, our sense of right and wrong in proper focus. This war has made it almost impossible for many of us. I am very much afraid that the likes of Songmy is but a portent of things to come.

People vs. Stones

Among the great ideas that our people have given to the world is that of the sanctity of human life. For us it has always remained an inviolable principle, even though the nations around us refused to recognize its efficacy. For generations we stood as an island of activity amidst an ocean of barbarism due to the fact that long ago we had accepted the Divine principle of the right to life. No human being could ever deny another human that right; and our ancient Sanhedrin, our famed court of law, hesitated to invoke the death penalty even when warranted. The Talmud infers that through the entire history of the Jewish courts of law, capital punishment was never meted out. Better to proclaim the accused innocent on the slightest technicality than risk condemning to death a possibly innocent man, even though the bulk of the evidence proclaimed his guilt.

In this, the seventh decade of the 20th century, we would like to think that some of what we have been preaching and living for thousands of years has started to take effect in the world at large. But understandably we have our doubts.

It was therefore with a resigned sadness that I read the following not too long ago:

"The Vietnam wars of this century, involving Japanese, French, Americans and Vietnamese, have left more than ruins in Indochina. These ruins we could do without; but there is one ruin that we cannot do without. It is of course the ancient city of Angkor Wat, potentially endangered by the Cambodian war. This magnificent temple-city marks the Khmer civilization which flourished from 800 to 1400 A.D. It is one of the truly great architectural wonders of all time and thus it must be preserved. Angkor Wat is a priceless heritage that must be there for future generations, when peace comes again to all of Indochina."

Well, this piece of misplaced journalistic sentiment speaks for itself. Never mind the murdered civilians, never mind the bombed out villages; forget about about the burned children, forget about the dead soldiers of a half dozen nations. Only remember not to destroy the bricks and stone of Angkor Wat.

When will we learn that stones can be replaced but a human life can never be replaced? Shall the day ever come when the world will realize that people are more important than buildings?

Yom Kippur is a time when we implore God for another year of life. We are reminded once again of the transitory nature of our stay on this earth and thus each minute that we have becomes so much more precious.

Perhaps the leaders of the world should join us in the prayer for all life, and not be so concerned about the Angkor Wats of our earth.

We can restore ruins. Can we do the same for human life?

Who Shall Live; Who Shall Die

The Persian Gulf War will not end in a few days, or even in a few weeks. The casualties to date have been relatively light, although I hesitate to characterize any casualty as light. If you are the mother or the brother of a young marine whose body pieces have been exploded across the Saudi sands, then the words "light casualties" do not apply; you and yours have paid the ultimate price for a United States policy that is determined to eliminate the Iraqi military threat. Ultimately we have to "pay the piper" and we are paying with the coin of young lives. Surely no one deluded themselves into thinking that war can be fought without blood.

But how much blood is necessary? Our Generals have outlined a battle plan that calls for two major phases: an airwar to destroy all strategic targets including Scud missile emplacements, ammunition and fuel depots, airfields and communications as well as a softening up of Hussein's formidable infantry and armor; followed by a ground invasion. Von Klausewitz himself posits that only ground forces can occupy and hold territory.

Slowly the air sorties are having the desired effect, though not as quickly as we would like. But each passing day brings renewed terror to the Israeli population who are undergoing their own horrible version of the "London Blitz," along with the Saudi population. One of the most bizarre consequences of the Scud missile attacks is the "twinning" of Tel-Aviv and Riyadh as sister cities in suffering.

The Israeli Defense Forces would not have given Iraq five months notice to carefully and systematically prepare for war, nor years to perfect their capability for gas, biological and nuclear warfare, nor the opportunity to protect their air force and their troops in specially designed concrete and steel bunkers, nor the option to send missiles into Tel-Aviv and Haifa without the threat of immediate and devastating retaliation from which there would be no Iraqi recovery. Israel would not have sold sophisticated armaments and technology to a future enemy and underestimated his potential for aggression after observing his dress rehearsal against Iran.

However, our generals insist that Kuwait can only be liberated by ground troops. But Edward Luttwak, military analyst, has challenged this assumption: a protracted air war can succeed in cutting off all supplies to the Republican Guard entrenched in Kuwait. Convoys bringing food, water and ammunition can easily be destroyed by the Allied airforces, as well as tank columns and armored personnel carriers on the move. That would leave the Iraqi occupation army with three choices: retreat, surrender, or die. Then the Kuwaitis can liberate Kuwait in a mopping-up action aided by their coalition brothers and supported by U.S. air and ground firepower from the distance. There is no good reason for tens of thousands of young Americans to die in the desert in close combat with Iraqi troops whose primary goal is to kill "satanic" Americans and Israelis. Saddam Hussein is already a hero in some quarters, particularly among the Palestinians who cheer as the Scud missiles plow into Tel-Aviv and clamor for a gas attack. Hussein has attacked Israel, killed and wounded Jews, and the Israelis "haven't dared" to respond. He has invaded Saudi Arabia, liberated the town of Khafji (at least for a few hours), killed Americans and Saudis, and he has captured western pilots. He would love for the western allies to advance into Kuwait where his huge army waits to die in glorious battle with the infidel so that paradise may be gained and everlasting fame in the Arab world attained.

We do not have to fight this war according to his plan. Rather we need to consider a plan that will achieve the most conclusive results with the least amount of American blood spilled. Iraq's military strength can be significantly reduced from the air if not practically eliminated. All we need is patience and resolve. Unfortunately our attention span is too short; we grow impatient much too quickly. If American policy has precluded turning Baghdad, Basra and Mosul into desert dust (as we did to Hiroshima, Nagasaki and Dresden when we weighed American lives against Japanese or German lives), then we are forced to wait for Iraqi capitulation much longer than we would prefer. And if the life of one young American can be saved with this approach, to say nothing of thousands of other lives, then it shall be worth our wait.

Letter from Gen. Norman Schwartzkopf
25 March 1991

Dear Rabbi Konovitch,

I want to express my sincere thanks for your letter voicing support for our valiant troops. The tremendous outpouring of encouragement by the American people has been the foundation and driving force behind our success in both Operation Desert Shield and Operation Desert Storm.

You and thousands like you have provided us the strength and determination to liberate Kuwait and fulfill the United Nations Resolutions. It is because of this visible demonstration of concern for our soldiers, sailors, airmen, marines and coastguardsmen that we in the military are proud to be serving our country and its citizens.

Again, thank you as we look forward to the day when our last servicemember returns to the shores of our great nation.

Sincerely,

H. Norman Schwarzkopf
General, U.S. Army

PART III
THE JEWISH DEFENSE LEAGUE

The Super-Patriots

My friends, anyone can wave a flag, wear a badge and call himself a patriot. What really counts is how we act behind that flag, what we do to bring honor to that badge.

We suffer from the super-patriots. There are those among us who suffer from an inferior identity. These people feel that deep inside they are Jewish cowards. That the world knows the secret of their cowardice and laughs at them. These are the people who are ashamed of their ancestors; who are ashamed that Jews allowed themselves to be gassed and allowed themselves to be shot; who actually blame the Jews for being killed and not the Nazis for killing them. These people wish to prove to the world that the Jew is not going to take it lying down. Jewish identity must be strengthened.

Accordingly these super-patriots invaded the offices of Arabic Palestinian organizations here in New York and proceeded to smash a few heads.

The Israeli government is suddenly incapable of handling its own affairs. It needs the help of a few misguided Jews to act as vigilantes here in New York City, thousands of miles from the problem.

These are not Jewish patriots, even with the flags and with the arm bands. These are Jewish criminals. These monsters should not be applauded in our communities; they should be condemned as the criminals that they are. Imagine, in the name of Jewish patriotism violent criminal attacks are perpetrated.

And I have heard talk from a few people that this was a proper course of action to take. "Show them that the Jews can hit also."

Yes we showed them. We showed them that we as Jews can come down to the level of the basest of criminals. We showed them that we can be as vicious and intolerant as the next fellow. We showed them that if Arab guerillas could bomb and machine gun a bus load of innocent children, then Jewish guerillas could also beat up innocent people. An eye for an eye, a tooth for a tooth, a disgrace for a disgrace.

We are outraged when Arab terrorists attack Israeli citizens in their own country and especially in other countries. Shall we not be equally as outraged when Jewish terrorists do the same? The world was horrified when Jews were attacked in Greece. Shall they not be horrified when Arabs are attacked in New York?

First of all, no Jew who is not an Israeli citizen has a right to even talk for Israeli political or military policy, much less act for it.

And secondly, all of us, as Israeli Jews or American Jews, have a choice to make. Either we shall come down to the animalistic level of our adversaries, or we shall strive to maintain our standards in the hope that some day we shall bring others up to those standards.

We have lost much throughout our history in physical and material terms. But one thing we never lost was our basic ethical standards.

The super-patriots, carrying American flags or Israel flags, are a threat to survival of our humanity. They are tearing our country apart, they are tearing our Jewish people apart.

Militants, Extremists and Defenders

One of the most difficult stigmas that the Jew has been trying to rid himself of is that of the people who never strike back, the people who allow themselves to be led to the slaughter. Our whole history has been characterized, by Gentile historians that is, as a series of pogroms and persecutions that found the Jew getting his neck on the chopping block or trudging into the gas chambers without so much as a cry raised in protest, or a fist raised in defiance.

How wrong they were, those nearsighted recorders, who thought that the Jew was acting in this finest Christian tradition when he turned the other cheek. What a triumph for the people who gave to the world the "savior" of mankind. How nice indeed for the Jews to accept the responsibility of fulfilling this noble Christian doctrine. It left the rest of Christianity free to do as they would. And do as they would they did.

How this shameful canard grated in the maws of so many Jews! Had the world forgotten the heroes of the Warsaw ghetto? Didn't they remember how a handful of brave young Jews fought the Nazi war machine to a standstill? Had the history book already buried the names of Samson, David, Bar Kochba and the countless of others who rose to defend our people and our homeland in times of crisis?

In every generation we have had the defenders of our people and our faith. In Spain and in Italy, in Poland and in Hungry, in Israel and in America. Even in our day there arises a group of Jewish individuals who call themselves the Jewish Defense League. Are they the descendants of the warriors of David? Are they fair to the partisans of Poland? Are they the sons of the Shomrim of the Emek? I suggest that they are neither Jewish nor defenders of anything.

Not Jewish because Jews seek to build bridges of communication between peoples and races, not destroy them. And not defenders because they do not defend us against our so called enemies. Rather they attack, creating enemies from our friends, and drive away those we seek to befriend.

Everyone of us condemned the black militant groups as extremist peddlers of mistrust and hate. Can we, in good conscience, now condone a group, albeit Jewish, that stands for the very same things? All militant radicals are dangerous and must be condemned no matter who they are. They will only succeed in arousing the fears and prejudices of men, prejudices that we have been striving for so long to erase.

Perhaps, as Jews, we have a right to be over-sensitive to contemporary political and racial movements. Our recent history has sharpened our senses to the point where we jump at the slightest noise. But we have no right to over-react. We have been the victims of over-reaction in the past; we dare not become its perpetrators in the present.

Defend our people? By all means. Not by isolating us from other segments of our society. Not by destroying the unity within our own ranks. Not by driving a wedge between people. Rather by breaking down the walls that separate us from ourselves and from others. There will be enough battles to fight in the future. Let us not waste our energy tilting with windmills.

J.D.L. Revisited
May 22, 1971

When our American forefathers looked for an apt phrase to inscribe on the liberty bell they turned to the Bible. "Proclaim liberty throughout the land to all its inhabitants."

We Jews were quick to realize at the beginnings of our national history that liberty is the inherent right of every citizen in a free society. Liberty denied to one person is liberty denied to all. If just one of us is enslaved, we are all enslaved.

And so it was fitting that when the Anti-Defamation League was formed to fight for Jewish rights, our fight was not limited to Jews. As an oppressed minority group we understood that if we are going to achieve our full measure of freedom then all minority groups will have to achieve the same. Freedom in America was never strictly a Jewish cause, or an Irish cause, or a black cause. It was an American cause. If we are free in America today, we are free because we are American and not because we are Jewish, Irish or black.

How can we deny to others what we as Jews have valiantly struggled for? Very emphatically our Torah declares freedom for "all inhabitants." And the struggle for their freedom is not just their struggle. It is clearly our struggle.

Certainly we understand that our freedom takes priority for our energy. Only free people can help others to be free. But let us not forget that the struggle doesn't stop with ourselves. To limit our efforts to ourselves, as some of our people have suggested, is not only contrary to the letter and the spirit of our law, but will eventually undermine our own freedom.

It was therefore not so surprising to me when last year Leonard Bernstein hosted a fundraising party to raise bail for the arrested black panthers. There was a principle involved.

The right to bail is a cornerstone of our free law. It may not be denied. And you may recall the uproar in Jewish circles. Most people simply could not distinguish between the principle of law involved and the basic philosophy of the black panthers. Rights are something reserved for fine upstanding, normal, conservative, G-d fearing, respectable citizens. Not for those black misfits who just don't fit the description of some people's idea of American.

But the more perceptive citizens understood that basically this was an important issue. One that had serious implications for all minority groups. Only the question remained that perhaps the maestro could involve himself in causes a bit closer to home. Surely we have not exhausted our own priority Jewish causes.

Several months ago just such a Jewish cause presented itself. An almost identical cause. A certain Avraham Hershkowitz was being held for trial. He was charged with conspiracy to hijack an Arab plane. The cause of Avraham Hershkowitz was certainly as misguided and as lunatic as that of the black panthers. But his right to bail was certainly as important as theirs.

I recall being terribly bothered by this question. Where was the maestro Bernstein and his friends now? Surely one of their own is as important as the panthers. If it is only a question of the principle involved and not the political ideology, surely Avraham Hershkowitz has just as much right to the principle as anyone else?

The activities of the black panthers and the activities of Avraham Hershkowitz and his cohorts are to be equally condemned. They are repugnant to everything that we stand for as Jews and as Americans. But their right under the law must be upheld by everyone of us. That is what democracy is all about.

However, it is very difficult for many people to separate the principle from the ideology. It is one thing to petition for the right to bail. It is quite another thing to be asked to raise that bail. Actively participating in raising the bail may imply an identification with the cause of the accused. According to our own Jewish instincts the right to bail is a cause that we must all struggle for regardless of who the accused is. Jew, gentile, black, white, it makes no difference. But the raising of that bail is an individual's choice, subject to his own personal feelings and persuasions.

No one can be asked to compromise his own principles by actively participating in a cause that he is opposed to. Raising bail may demonstrate just such a participation.

It was not surprising therefore, that when the J.D.L. approached the New York Board of Rabbis for $65,000 in bail money for Avraham Hershkowitz they were turned down. The 900 member Rabbis from the New York area refused to be associated in any way with these criminal activities. And being Jewish does not make a criminal any less of a criminal.

The response from the J.D.L. was one that horrified the entire Jewish community. A squad of 25 hoodlums smashed their way into the office of the N.Y. Board on April 28th. They broke T.V. and radio sets and tape recorders. They cut telephone wires, ripped phones out of the wall, scattered papers and files. They made a shambles out of that office. But the several thousand dollars of damage was not the worst part of it.

I spoke with Rabbi Harold Gordon, the executive vice president. He was in the office at the time of the raid. When he and members of the staff tried to stop the intruders they were told they had orders. Orders to demolish the place and to take care of anyone who stood in their way.

Friends, I have spoken out against the activities of the J.D.L. right from the beginning. But for a long time now I have been quiet. I had realized that to constantly attack them would only give them undeserved attention. The constant debates concerning their activities were having a terrible effect on our community. People were being diverted from the real issues, the important issues of the day. Congregants would come to argue, to take a stand one way or another concerning the J.D.L. And they would go home convinced that they had accomplished something for the Russian Jews. Debates concerning the J.D.L. were becoming counter-productive.

But they didn't go away by themselves. And people continued to sympathize with their rather romantic, so-called defense of Jewish people.

Well my friends, now you see what they mean by defense. Are we being defended when Jews attack fellow Jews? Are we being defended when Jews threaten other Jews? For this we don't need the J.D.L. For this we have the Ku Klux Klan or the John Birch society or the American Nazi Party.

I must tell you that even amongst my colleagues, sympathy for the J.D.L. had been growing. Growing, that is, until now. Not one Rabbi that quietly supported J.D.L. in the past, is continuing to do so. We have finally seen them for what they are. The romantic veil has been parted to reveal a gang of misguided Jewish hoodlums.

Some of our people still try to separate the general philosophy of the J.D.L. from their activities at the N.Y. Board. Let us understand once and for all that what happened at the N.Y. Board was not an unfortunate accident. It was a logical consequence of what has been going on in J.D.L. all along. Do we have to wait until someone is killed before we wake up? Violence cannot be meted out in controlled doses. It has a way of running away with those who use it.

We have been polarized long enough because of the J.D.L. It is time to come back together again and devote our time and energy, and our words, to the important issues of our day, in a productive manner. We created the J.D.L. and we can lay it to rest.

Yes, we created the monster. We saw the vacuum in the Jewish community, but we did not step forward to fill it in a responsible manner. We have realized the inequities in our major Jewish organizations for some time now. We have understood the necessity for reordering our priorities in the Jewish community for many years. But we were too quiet. We were too still. And we allowed the JDL to fill the quiet with their own twisted brand of noise. Their ends, even if one were to grant that they have achieved anything, can never justify their means.

We have had our warning. Either we will gather to take care of our own interests, or the lunatics will take care of them for us; and I am afraid they will take care of us together.

In case the N.Y. Board incident did not convince you that our best interests were not being served then perhaps the Italian-

Jewish alliance did. In a final act of "defense" Meir Kahane and Joe Columbo joined forces. The Italian mafia and the Jewish mafia have been joined into unholy wedlock.

Can anyone in his right mind construe this unbelievable move as in the best interests of the Jewish community? I can only say that at last the JDL has the proper bedmate.

It is high time that Jewish causes should be truly defended and not destroyed. We cannot let a lunatic fringe speak and act on our behalf. We must be rid of them once and for all. But we dare not create another vacuum. You and I must step forward and speak responsibly for the Jewish community. The time for standing on the sidelines is over. It is we who must become the true defenders of the Jewish cause.

Letter from Meir Kahane
June 25, 1970

President and Chairman of the Board
of the Laurelton Jewish Center
and Editor of the Center's Bulletin
137th Avenue and 228th Street
Laurelton, New York 11413

Gentlemen:

The following is our reply to a rather shocking attack on Jewish patriots by Rabbi B. Konowich in the LJC Bulletin of June 19th.

I believe that both courtesy and fair play call for the Rabbi to reply and hope that this will either take the form of a reprint of this letter or, better still, tender an opportunity for a JDL speaker to present the case for these people at a speaking date in your synagogue.

The attack on the "super patriots" by Rabbi Konowich in the June 19th issue of the Bulletin is hardly a new one. In general, those leaders who do little must explain away the actions of others who do a great deal for the Jewish people and will attempt to accomplish this by deprecating the actions of the activists.

Thus, we find that those who attacked the Arab office in New York City, are "Jewish criminals" and are called "murderers" to be condemned—to be condemned for beating up "innocent people." The Rabbi is either ignorant or worse. To call the local office, to call members of the local Al Fatah office, the office that raises funds for the murderers of Jewish children, "innocent people" is outlandish and inexplicable.

To call such actions "vicious and intolerant" and to equate them with the act of murder in Israel, is to see no difference

72

between Arab murder of Israelis and Israeli retaliation which results in the death of Arabs.

While Rabbi Konowich deplores the concept of an eye for an eye, it is this concept which is the cornerstone of Israeli foreign policy. If Rabbi Konowich disapproves of that, he does so because his liberalism transcends his Jewishness. Those who assaulted the Arabs were not doing so as Israelis; they did it as Jews in retaliation for the death of other Jews and there are no boundary lines when it comes to the Jewish people.

We do not begrudge Rabbi Konowich his do-nothingness: we simply suggest that he refrain from attacking those who care enough to act.

In conclusion, I would like to quote the following attack by the Jewish establishment on other "criminals." "These despicable criminals have put us in jeopardy. It is our bounden duty to treat them likewise." The year was 1944, the "criminals" were Hakin and Betsoury who assassinated Lord Moyne. Today, they are heroes; but it doesn't discard the fact that in every generation, the timid, the comfortable and the myopic have always attacked the minority of avengers.

With Love of Israel,

Meir Kahane
National Chairman

Who's Afraid of the J.D.L.?

Each year that well known exponent of Arab-Israeli brother-hood comes to Miami to raise money and public consciousness for the "Kach" cause. And each year Meir Kahane has a difficult time finding a forum for his viewpoint; synagogue after synagogue refuses to allow him to speak. Synagogue boards spend more time condemning him than planning how to help the State of Israel. National organizations spend more time devising schemes to block him than they do encouraging aliyah to Eretz Yisrael.

What are we afraid of? If Meir is Menachem's true inheritor than we should be able to tell after several minutes of his rhetoric. And if his thinking is closer to the Mufti's then this too will become apparent. An open exchange of coherent ideas between intelligent people never harmed anyone. It is only the repression of ideas and their free interchange that harm our society. Only in a totalitarian state is a person prohibited from thinking for himself. Only in a repressive society is the establishment afraid of a "contra philosophy."

If Meir Kahane espouses a philosophy contrary to the heart and soul of the Jewish people, then he will soon be relegated to the footnotes of history. If, however, he touches a receptive chord, then he deserves recognition. Historically the Jewish people have always wavered between peace and war. In the end we have been guided by more than the contingencies of the moment, more than emotion, more than "Realpolitik." Our greatest leaders have led us through our finest hours guided by the time-tested principles of our Torah. Unfortunately those principles are open to interpretation from every segment of the political spectrum.

Each can and does quote scripture for his own purpose. Unfortunately it is only in retrospect that we learn the real truth. Only after the day has been saved, or conversely, after

THE JEWISH DEFENSE LEAGUE

the damage has been done do we learn which decisions were indeed correct.

At the time, who could really know how history would treat the raiders of Deir Yassin or the attackers of the Altalena? Who could know if Ben Gurion and Ben Zvi; or Begin and Stern were the true inheritors of Hezekiah and Hyrcanus? Only history is the final arbiter of the truth, but unfortunately only after the fact.

We must make our decisions here and now. If we are right, if we are in the mainstream of Jewish History, if we are properly buttressed by traditional principles, then history will judge us positively. But if we are wrong, if our decisions are narrowly based on the exigencies of the moment, if our actions reflect little light and much heat, then not only will we be condemned by our history, but much worse, we will do ourselves irreparable harm.

In the year 132 CE, Simon Bar Kosiba led a revolt against the Roman occupation forces in Judea. Rabbi Akiva proclaimed him as "King and Messiah." Three and one half years later Julius Severus and his legions destroyed Betar and Bar Kochba and the independent Jewish State. It took almost 2,000 years for the Jewish people to establish another independent Jewish State. Rabbi Akiva and Bar Kochba were opposed by moderates who counseled restraint, and diplomatic accommodation with the Roman rulers of the entire known world. The "hawks" carried the day, and the result was decimation for Judea on a scale never seen before: tens of thousands dead and Jewish slaves in such large numbers that they could be bought for a "horse's ration."

To this very day we are not quite sure about Rabbi Akiva's decision. However one thing is clear: the consequences of his rhetoric were terrifying. Right or wrong, the fact remains: Israel's independence was destroyed.

1986 is no less complicated and fraught with dangers than 132. We too must deal with world powers that always place their own interests and needs above ours.

We too must walk that fine line between accommodation and capitulation. And the last thing we need is to be manipulated by modern messianists. Hopefully we have learned something from our past political mistakes. We are a nation made wise by experience. By now we should have a sixth sense that guides us toward the truth.

If Meir Kahane speaks the truth, if his thinking is rigorous, if his argument is logical, if his program is politically viable, if his principles are Jewish, if his goals are survival, if his ultimate objective is peace, then let us accept him as a true leader. If he speaks falsehood then let him be rejected once and for all as a "False Prophet."

But in a free society he has the right to be heard.

And so do we.

PART IV

THE ODYSSEY OF SOVIET JEWRY

3½ Million = 25% of World Jewry

Jewish identity has been reborn in the Soviet Union. Russian Jews have found the strength to publicly petition the government for the right to emigrate to their land of Israel. The truth is out in the open for all to know: Conditions are unbearable; the Russian Jews want out!

The most recent events in Russia, namely the Leningrad hijacking trial, are a study in present Russian attitudes. They demonstrate to us very graphically how disturbed the Russians are about their Jews, and to what length they will go to silence them. The whole world is aware of the fact that the entire fiasco was manufactured by the KGB, the Russian secret police, that in a desperate attempt to frighten Russian Jews into silence, this trial was staged.

But for once the traditional scare tactics of the KGB have failed. Instead of frightening the Russian Jews into silence they have made them even more determined to raise their voices and secure their freedom. And around the world the same has been true. Instead of cowering before the Russian threats, world Jewry is crying out even louder. And if you want to know if our efforts have borne any fruit then just consider the recent sentences handed down by the Russian courts. Two Jews were saved because of the cry heard 'round the world. Can anyone remember the last time anything was able to influence the Russian mind to such an extent?

Yes we have already accomplished much. We have alerted the whole world as to the real situation in Russia. No one can come and say "We didn't know. We weren't aware of the situation." Our job is to make sure that the world continues to be apprised of the situation.

We want everyone to know that the Jewish people are threatened with another holocaust. And if the world insists on remaining silent, as they did just 30 years ago, then the blood of Russian Jewry will be on their hands. If they will not join us in protest then they shall surely share the terrible consequences of their silence.

And our task is to personally remain informed of the situation. Each one of us must become a keeper of the historical truth; each of us must become a witness to the fact. We will not allow the truth to be hidden from the world as it was during World War II. The Russian government will not be allowed to sweep the facts under the rug as the Germans did until it was too late.

And finally it is our task to make our presence felt. The Jews in the Soviet Union must know that we are with them. That we will not remain silent. That we will not leave any stone unturned in our effort to free them. I don't think we shall ever know what this is worth to our Russian brethren in terms of spirit, in terms of morale.

But most important is our physical presence, here, in New York, in London, in Paris, in Rome, around the world, in front of the Russian embassies, in front of the television and movie cameras, in the newspapers, and in the magazines.

Thank God we are not without influence in high places. But the influence of our people depends a good deal on the amount of public opinion we can arouse. Every added face in front of the Russian embassy means more weight behind the demands of our influential leaders.

No one listens to individuals in this country. They listen to numbers, and the greater the numbers the more keenly they listen.

Each of us counts. Every time one of us decides that his presence isn't important, that he doesn't make any real difference, every time such a decision is made our cause is weakened.

We have reached a turning point. If we can keep up the pressure; if we can continue to raise our voices; if we are persistent; if we refuse to grow tired, then that Soviet Iron Curtain will crack. And then the final chapters of the modern exodus will be written for our people.

Am Yisroel Chai. The people of Israel live. But only if each and every one of you will it. Unless you join your voice to ours, unless you join your presence to ours, then the blood of our Russian brethren will surely be on our hands. We have heard enough, we have debated enough, we have been outraged enough. Now is the time to rise and to act.

The Lord give us the strength to persist, and we shall save our Russian brothers.

Let My People Go

I have often said that the Seder is a stage upon which we are asked to play the role of slaves in the process of achieving freedom. The success of the Seder depends on how carefully we can follow the script of the Haggadah and play the parts of our ancient ancestors.

None of us have any difficulty in playing the part of freemen. We were born free, in a country that has always recognized us as a free and equal people under the law.

Or we have lived in a free country long enough to forget the days of our persecution and degradation. Freedom is a familiar role, one we slip into quite easily and one that we are quite comfortable with. It is the role of slaves that challenges our imaginations and requires a great deal of thought and understanding to play.

But for our brethren behind the iron curtain, the roles are reversed. For them the part of slaves is an easy one to play. It isn't even acting, it is imitating reality, a reality that relegates them to the roles of second class citizens. The role of free men is one they find hard to imagine, and the script of their Haggadah reflects a freedom that is merely an elusive dream, a dream that is fast disappearing.

Eighteen Jewish families in the Georgian sector of the U.S.S.R. appealed to the U.N. last year in the following letter:

"We, 18 religious Jewish families of Georgia, request you to help us leave for Israel. Each of us, upon receiving an invitation from a relative in Israel, obtained the necessary questionnaires from the authorized U.S.S.R. agencies and filled them out. Years have gone by and permission for departure has not been granted. We see no written replies. No one explains anything. No one cares about our fate.

"They say there is a total of 12 million Jews in the world. But he errs who believes that there are only 12 million. For with

82

those who pray for Israel are hundreds of millions who did not live to this day, who were tortured to death, who are no longer here. They marched shoulder to shoulder with us, unconquered and immortal, those who handed down to us the traditions of struggle and faith.

"That is why we want to go to Israel. It is incomprehensible that in the 20th century people can be prohibited from living where they wish to live.

"We will wait months and years, we will wait all our lives if necessary, but we will not renounce our faith or our hopes.

"We believe: Our prayers have reached G-d.

"We know: Our appeals have reached humanity. For we are asking little. Let us go to the land of our forefathers."

The Seder is over, and the acting is over. We are back in the familiar role of free men. Our brothers in Russia are back in the familiar role of slaves. If the exodus does not begin for them soon, we shall not have any Russian Jewish brothers to even remember next Passover.

Protest. Demonstrate. Cry out with all your might: Let my people go.

"The Day They Marched Out of the Synagogue"

The first day of Rosh Hashanah, in the year 5732, was a milestone in the history of the Jewish community of Laurelton, and indeed in the history of the Jewish community of New York. In a most unique and impressive manner, approximately two thousand congregants of our Center demonstrated their unflagging support for our brothers behind the Iron Curtain.

To underscore our concern for the welfare of our Russian brethren, the traditional Rosh Hashanah service was brought out into the middle of town, and the shofar, ancient symbol of our struge for freedom, was sounded for all to hear.

It was an awe inspiring sight. Two thousand congregants streaming out of the synagogue in their talleisim, with dignity and solemnity, following their Rabbi on a march into modern Jewish history.

There wasn't a Jew in sight who didn't feel great pride. Pride in being part of this inspiring demonstration. Pride in being a member of the Laurelton Jewish Center. Pride in being a Jew concerned for the fate of his fellow Jew.

And by the end of Rosh Hashanah, there wasn't a Jew in New York who wasn't excited about the events at the Laurelton Jewish Center, because five newspapers, four radio stations, and most important, four television networks on the early and late news covered this amazing demonstration.

Our presence in such great numbers, and our prayers, captured public attention in a manner that it has never been captured before. We may feel certain that the news of our assembly penetrated the Iron Curtain itself and has given the morale of the Russian Jews a new lift.

I have no doubt that we were also given a spiritual "lift." Our prayers took on a deeper meaning when we translated their beautiful sentiments into beautiful action.

We cannot expect to single-handedly become the saviors of the Soviet Jews. But we do expect to be a substantial part of the effort to save them. And on Rosh Hashanah we were not only a significant part of that effort, but we led the way. In the words of the Director of the New York Board of Rabbis, . . . "with the proper zeal and imagination we have achieved a great deal in the area of Soviet Jewry."

It was indeed high time that someone demonstrated to the Jewish community that there is a highly effective and responsible alternative to throwing rocks and exploding bombs.

You my friends, you who followed me out of the synagogue and into the streets, you can be very proud of yourselves indeed.

We will never let the world forget that 2½ million of our brethren are deprived of their basic human rights in the Soviet Union. We will not allow the world to sweep the facts under the rug as they did during World War II. We will not allow them to plead ignorance to the problem as they did during the holocaust. We shall remain keepers of the historical fact. And we shall remain an ever present bone in the throat of the world, until our people achieve freedom. It shall never be said of us that the Russians were the Jews of Silence, because we were the Jews of silence. Our voices will never be stilled until the last Jew who wishes to leave is granted his exit visa.

As part of our continuing effort I would ask all of you to address special Rosh Hashanah greetings to the Jewish communities of Russia. The proper addresses appear above. Our Soviet brothers will be very happy and proud to hear from us personally.

And above all, in this new year we shall continue to pray and act on behalf of peace and freedom for our brothers everywhere.

Freedom now!

Summit Sunday: A March Into History

The word went out from a little man who is one of the giants of our time: Anatoly Sharansky called for 400,000 Jews to demonstrate in Washington, DC, on the eve of the Reagan-Gorbachev summit meeting. One free Jew for every Soviet brother or sister who languishes in the limbo of the gulag society. If there were any doubts about the efficacy of such tactics, they were quickly and effectively dispelled when Sharansky reminded us that he is alive and free today only because Jews around the world never allowed the Russian authorities to think that he was forgotten.

Constant public demonstrations of solidarity for close to a decade prevented his permanent disappearance into a government asylum or a Siberian labor camp.

Now the fate of all Russian Jewry hangs in the balance. Encouraged by the policy of "Glasnost," the Jews of the free world had one last chance to redeem what was left of the ravaged Soviet Jewish community, before years of religious and cultural deprivation, political oppression and the inevitable assimilation took their final toll. There might never be another opportunity because the Russian Jewish community would all but cease to exist.

We worked and hoped for a respectable showing. But not in our wildest imagination could we have anticipated that close to a quarter of a million Jews would assemble in front of the Capitol in Washington, DC, on a cold winter's day in December. From Hawaii and Alaska they came; from South American and Israel; from almost every state in the union; from small towns and big cities. Some 1,000 people from Florida formed one of the largest contingents. With our Rabbis and synagogue leaders we came; with our political and community leaders we marched, banners proudly identifying our organizations, but all enveloped in the one banner of "Let My People Go."

The weather was perfect as if Joshua himself had once again demanded the cooperation of the elements. Our Florida delegation, buried under layers of unaccustomed winter clothing, were warmed by the shared camaraderie, the sense of urgent purpose and the overwhelming feeling of being part of 'Klal Yisroel," the worldwide community of Jewish people.

We gathered as one, we *were* one. One heart; one mind; one purpose. It was a once-in-a-lifetime experience, never to be forgotten, to be retold around future Seder tables for years to come; how the modern Exodus was precipitated by the largest gathering of Jewish people in modern times.

"Summit Sunday" was one of the greatest gatherings ever seen in Washington. It may have been the biggest gathering of Jewish people since Moses rallied the people at Mt. Sinai some thirty-five hundred years ago; and as with Sinai, every Jew was represented in Washington. Each of us brought the hopes, the dreams and the commitment of every member of our community. Each of us realized that we were on the front lines in the battle for Jewish survival. In the face of such a confrontation with the future, all the minor problems of the day, the wind chill factor, the bus transportation, the charter airplane schedules, all faded away. Left was the overwhelming sense of fulfillment of a holy mission. For every Jew, every lover of freedom, every advocate of human rights, Washington was the place to be on December 6, 1987, the 15th of Kislev, one and one half weeks before Chanukah, our "Holiday of Freedom."

Throughout the day, one thought kept surfacing: Almost fifty years ago the survival of millions of Jews was at stake. Had the free world been more demonstrative, had the Jewish people been more insistent, had we mustered the courage of our convictions to actively and unequivocally demand the rescue of European Jewry, perhaps the Holocaust would not have occurred. Had the Jews of New York and Miami and Havana demanded the release of their brothers and sisters on the ship St. Louis; had they paralyzed the piers, chained themselves to the docking lines, invaded the government chambers, and marched en masse to Roosevelt's White House, and Batista's and Bru's Palacio Presidencial, perhaps we would not be reciting a yearly kaddish for the martyrs. Perhaps our Yizkor would be a yearly remembrance of Jewish history's finest moment instead of its most tragic.

Courage and sacrifice are the price of Jewish survival.

Soviet Jews: Israeli Citizens

The recent events in the Soviet Union constitute nothing less than a major revolution in governmental policy. Not since the Bolsheviks have we witnessed such an earthshaking transformation. Communism, mixed with Perestroika, seems to be producing a Glasnost that is "democratizing Russia." A by-product of this new chemistry is a new freedom for Russian Jews. The proverbial iron curtain has opened; some 30–40,000 Russian Jews are expected to emigrate this year alone.

It is imperative that Jewish philanthropic organizations prepare financially to help our brothers and sisters from Russia resettle in the free world.

But the destination for Russian Jews in the free world must be Israel, and it is to Israel where all funds for Russian Jewish resettlement must be sent. The Soviet Government grants emigration permits to its Jewish citizens with the proviso and understanding that they return to their national homeland, the State of Israel. Sending Russian Jews to Brighton Beach or to Miami, Florida, and not to Israel merely gives the Russian government a convenient excuse to stop Jewish emigration at any time with the claim that it was organized under a false pretext.

Certainly Russian Jews have a right to emigrate to the country of their choice, but for political reasons they should first embark at Tel-Aviv airport. If Israeli life doesn't agree with them; if they are not satisfied with the housing, the job training, employment opportunities, education for themselves and their children, and life in a Jewish country, then they are free to leave. But at their own expense; not at the expense of the world Jewish community.

Russian Jews clamored to leave the Soviet Union for years because of religious persecution. They yearned to be educated as Jews and to live in a Jewish atmosphere.

I submit that driving a taxi cab in Manhattan, disassociating from the Jewish community except for the representative of the Federation who issues the checks, never entering a synagogue, and eventually assimilating, is not what we had in mind.

In Russia, the Jewish population would have totally assimilated and disappeared in another generation. What is the point of bringing them to America to do the same? Only in Israel will they be assured of a Jewish existence. Only in Israel will the Russian Jews become Jewish. With the exception of some American day school and Yeshiva programs, Russian Jewish children in America are lost.

And if the Russian Jews fail to understand this, if the fabled "Goldeneh Medina" beckons so strongly, if independent Israeli life is too hard for people accustomed to be "taken care of" by a Communist State, then they are free to go. In good conscience we who have refused to make aliya may not dictate to others to live in Israel.

But neither should we encourage Russian Jews to leave Israel by making them a philanthropic "offer that can't be refused."

Our money for the resettlement of Russian Jews should be sent directly to the State of Israel. And we hope and pray that an infusion of Russian Jews into Israel will enrich the country with a major Aliya movement, and will at the same time preserve the great heritage of the Russian Jewish people.

PART V
ART, MUSIC AND POLITICS

Kinor David Stradivarius

One of the most difficult things on earth to accomplish effectively is to buy the right gift for the right person. How difficult this really is can be proven by standing at the exchange counter of any big department store after a major gift-oriented holiday, and observing the proceedings.

You never saw so many dissatisfied people in your life.

Imagine, then, how difficult it is to buy a gift for a State, particularly your very own Jewish State, on the momentous occasion of its 25th anniversary. How many different items might run through your mind:

Twenty-five F4 Phantom jets with shining blue Mogen David stars; an unlimited water supply for the Negev desert; a book on manners for every Israeli citizen below the age of ninety; one really good traffic cop for the corner of Jaffa and King George; Peace.

Recently Henryk Szeryng was having the same problem: What to give to the State of Israel in honor of its 25th anniversary? Mr. Szeryng is one of the world's leading violinists and his gift idea was one that was prompted by his own musical background.

Said he, "Israel has all kinds of Phantom jets and tanks, but it struck me last summer in Jerusalem that the people who have given to the world the greatest number of great fiddlers didn't possess a single important musical instrument for the benefit of its gifted sons."

Henryk Szeryng has such a violin, a 1734 Stradivarius that he originally purchased from conductor Charles Munch. The violin, valued at $60,000 dollars, will be renamed KINOR DAVID STRADIVARIUS, the lyre of David, and it will be available to young Israeli violinists to play. Meanwhile Mr. Szeryng will "make do" with his Guarnieri.

"So what," you say? Of all the things that Israel needs, the last thing she needs is a piece of brown wood with four strings. Is Moshe Dayan going to fiddle while Jerusalem burns? Couldn't Mr. Szeryng think of something more appropriate, more important? Is that what you say?

But wait a moment. Think. How beautiful indeed was Henryk Szeryng's gesture. Music is the world's only international language, and the Lord only knows how difficult it is for nations to communicate. Mr. Szeryng reminds us, there is a way to talk. If nations wish it, there need not be any language barrier. Perhaps the communication exemplified by music can indeed soothe the savage beast of war. Perhaps the violin can penetrate that which tanks cannot even attempt.

And with the proper, intelligent, rational communication, peace will come. King David eventually exchanged his sword for the lyre, his military manual for the Book of Psalms.

Peace will come and once more the sound of music will be heard in the land. And every person who sees that violin, who hears its sweet strains, will be reminded that the music of peace is more welcome to the human ear than the noises of war.

Peace will come. The violin says so.

Beethoven Has the Same Problem

On Wednesday, December sixteenth, the world celebrated the 200th anniversary of the great Ludwig van Beethoven. In the musical world this whole year has been devoted to honoring this most famous of all composers, through the performance of his works on a scale heretofore unheard of. Every great orchestra has devoted the better part of its seasonal offering to Beethoven, from the "Moonlight" to the "Eroica," from the sonatas to the string quartets.

He was born in Germany and made his home in Vienna, and within a few years he changed the face of music forever. Even in his own day it was recognized that no musician in the world came anywhere near him; and after his death in 1827 he came close to deification.

"This short, ill tempered, boorish, domineering, bad mannered, genius is still recognized as the greatest composer who ever lived." His accomplishments became all the more fantastic when one remembers that Beethoven was already afflicted by the onset of deafness at the age of 30, and his acknowledged greatest works were written afterward, in total silence!

In view of all this Howard Taubman of the Times recently quoted the following question: "Is Beethoven relevant 200 years after his birth?"

His answer was, that even to pose the question seems ludicrous, because Beethoven's works remain a staple of the repertory, and in the traditional hierarchy of values they represent one of the glories of civilization.

That same question has been posed to me a countless number of times. But not concerning Beethoven, but concerning the Jewish religion. "Is Judaism relevant some 4,000 years after its birth?"

And the answer is the same, and for the very same reasons.

As with the music of Beethoven, the Jewish religion continues to sum up the condition of man. Judaism continues to represent the very best in humanity: it continues to demand the very best from men.

Beethoven's ninth symphony is more than a piece of music. It is an ethos. The great composer preached a kind of democracy that would do away with class distinctions. He spoke musically of universal brotherhood. Many of his admirers saw in his works not just music but a set of ethics, a guide to the good life.

As long as civilization exists the ethical life will not go out of style. As long as life is valued, morality will still be relevant.

This is the sum total of Beethoven's relevancy in the modern world, indeed in any world. And this is a good part of the answer as to the relevancy of our own Jewish religion.

Does the love of one's fellow man ever go out of style? Does justice and righteousness and kindness ever become irrelevant? Does the truth ever become old fashioned?

The question of the relevancy of Judaism is even more ridiculous than the question of Beethoven's relevancy. Anyone who challenges the great composer's relevancy is probably a musical illiterate who never saw the inside of a Beethoven score, and who wouldn't recognize a Bethoven note if he fell over it.

And by the same token anyone who dismisses Judaism as old fashioned, anyone who challenges the relevancy of Judaism in the 20th century is probably a Jewish illiterate who would barely recognize the inside of a Siddur, and who wouldn't recognize a Jewish ethic even if he practiced it.

So you see that Beethoven and Judaism have another thing in common. Their potential audiences suffer from the same malady. Cerebral malnutrition. A dearth of education.

Howard Taubman says Beethoven will be around as long as men have ears to hear and hearts to inspire. Can anyone make the same claim for us? Who will predict an end to Jewish ignorance? Who will save us from the ignorant, irrelevant, relevance seekers?

Only you can.

Two Russian Pieces: Riggerman and Oistrakh

I. On Saturday evening, February 20, just before midnight, Leonid Riggerman touched down on free American soil. For three hours we had been milling about the Pan Am building, chatting with some of the hundreds of young people who had arrived for the great welcome home. As if from nowhere there had suddenly materialized a small group of musicians, and soon every one was singing and dancing, expressing their utter delight in the fact that the iron curtain had been breached again.

The sizeable contingent of police were smiling even in the face of this potentially volatile crowd. It was obvious where their sentiments lay.

I happened to glance at the schedule of incoming flights, on the big board across the room. In the space marked Aeroflot from Moscow, there was a big red sticker reading, "Save the Russian Jews."

Finally the big moment came and everybody rushed to the railings overlooking the customs area, in an effort to catch a first glimpse of Lenny.

And there he was, Russian hat and all, waving an Israeli and an American flag at the crowd. His bearded face sported the biggest smile I had ever seen.

They hustled him into a news conference and fifteen minutes later he came up to join his well wishers. It was a bit difficult to see him. Lenny Riggerman is a rather smallish man and he was practically buried by the ecstatic throng.

Finally one of the ever smiling policeman saved the day. He lifted Lenny onto his shoulders, flags and all.

And in an emotional voice, Leonid Riggerman, wearing a big blue yarmulka, thanked all the Jews of America who had worked so diligently to free him. He looked forward to the day when a crowd would gather every evening of every week to welcome Jews from the Soviet Union.

I shall never forget that beaming face of his. And when I recite the Amidah and mention the "resurrection of the dead," I shall see Leonid Riggerman in front of my eyes, truly resurrected from the dead.

II. On Sunday evening February 21, promptly at 8:30 P.M., Igor Oistrakh came out on the stage at the New York Philharmonic. For two hours previous to his scheduled performance, several dozen young people marched in protest of this concert. Young Jewish demonstrators have succeeded in bringing to a halt the cultural exchange between Russia and America, in an effort to call attention to the plight of the Soviet Jews. But we were a little surprised at the appearance of Jewish pickets on this particular evening. I engaged one of the pickets in conversation and I mentioned to him that Igor Oistrakh was himself a Jew.

His expression was one of surprise, but he quickly countered by explaining that Igor Oistrakh should refuse to play until the time comes when all Russian Jews are given their freedom.

The fact that Igor Oistrakh, the Jew, is one of the few people in Russia who is allowed freedom of artistic expression didn't seem to matter.

And as we stood there in front of Lincoln Center I was reminded of Pablo Casals and his self imposed, politically motivated, exile from Spain. He refused to play another note on Spanish soil until his people were free.

We were about to return to our seats when a passing woman turned to the pickets and loudly told them to "crawl back into the ovens." I was so taken aback that I couldn't even believe that the remark had been passed. But it had been heard by everyone around, including a nearby policeman who indicated with his club what he would have liked to answer.

It all seemed so unbelievable. A woman coming to Philharmonic Hall to listen to a Jewish violinist, and at the same time hurling Nazi epithets at a group of young Jews outside the hall.

Our Neo-Nazi wasn't alone, and she and her group sauntered through the crowd, gaining antagonists with every anti-semitic remark she made. Most people were too flabbergasted to say anything, but I couldn't refrain from a personal encounter, the likes of which I could never print.

We were finally in our seats awaiting the start of the concert, and for the first time I heard the following announcements: "We have reason to expect some minor disturbances during the evening. If you see anything suspicious, kindly raise your hand and our security guards will be right there."

With that Igor Oistrakh began to play, and after his first piece was over a surprise intermission was declared so that a contingent of police could search the hall for a bomb.

I can't say as the performer or the audience were ever quite at ease throughout the rest of the program.

At ten forty five, after four encores, Igor Oistrakh mopped his sweating brow, heaved a sigh of relief and left the stage, to a thunderous ovation.

But there was no smile on his face. For him the resurrection would have to wait.

Velázquez and Chanukah

In our overinflated economy most pocket books have been emptied. The big spenders just aren't spending anymore, to say nothing of the middle class spenders. And so it must come as quite a shock to most of us to read that a painting by the immortal Spanish painter Velazquez brought over five million dollars at a recent auction. This unbelievable price is a new record auction sale, but not long ago a private sale netted an art dealer even more. Six million dollars was paid to purchase a Leonardo Da Vinci.

Certainly no one can question the fact that the great masters have distilled from human experience the eternal spiritual and intellectual truths by which men fulfill themselves, to quote a distinguished art scholar. But what happens to these great works of art? What happens to the bits of our humanistic heritage preserved on a few square feet of pigment-covered canvas?

You can admire them in the Louvre, in the Prado, in the Rijksmuseum, or perhaps in the home of an affluent friend.

You can admire them from afar. You can delight in the superior technique, or the masterful use of colors. You may even be transfixed by the artist's idea as he expressed it on canvas.

But I doubt if you will identify with DaVinci, or Velazquez. I doubt if you will ever feel the way they felt, see the way they saw or experience what they experienced. Too many generations separate us. Too many conditions have changed in the world.

Now consider a Jewish artist. Better yet consider a Jewish art form, namely Jewish ceremonial art.

I happen to be addicted to antique Judaica. And just recently Aileen and I happened to stumble across a very interesting shop in Manhattan. The dealer had a beautiful collection of

100

menorahs, and since Chanukah is almost upon us we were interested. As with all great art the prices were skyhigh, but even so we were tempted.

But what would have happened to that magnificent 16th century menorah? Would we put it behind a glass case and admire it from afar? Would we merely marvel at the skill of the artisan, or the beauty of his creation?

No. This menorah would be taken out of its case and used. Used the way an unknown number of our ancestors had used it since the 16th century. That menorah would again burn brightly for eight days, in the very same way that it burned in the 16th century. Through it we would establish a link with the past. Through it we would be part of a tradition that started with the Maccabees in the year 165 BCE. It would link us to our very sources, and the spirit of that first Chanukah would live again. This feeling, even the great DaVinci couldn't give to me.

The whole idea is summed up in one sentence that we shall recite on Chanuka. "Bayamim ha-hem, bazman ha-zeh. "In those days as well as in our own day."

When those candles flame, the Maccabees live again. When we light the menorah, we live again. The world changes, but the Jewish spirit lives on.

For me Velazquez is dead, and I shall never experience what he experienced. But Mattathias is alive, and when I gaze upon the flaming menorah I will see what he saw and feel what he felt.

Wagner in Israel
January 30, 1992

The New York Times
229 West 43rd St.,
New York, N.Y. 10036

To the Editor:

Richard Taruskin's article, "Only Time will cover the Taint," (Jan. 26) cuts through the bombast surrounding the "Wagner in Israel" controversy, setting forth the real issue. As all philistines know, the opera isn't over until the fat lady sings; and in the Ring Cycle the fat lady never stops singing, except in Tel-Aviv where it will be a long time before she is even invited to begin.

However, Taruskin's analogy from "tref" (forbidden) pork to "tref" Wagner needs a bit of bolstering. Pork is forbidden for many reasons according to Jewish law. Its prohibition, as with all the laws of Kashrut, is meant to protect our physical and spiritual health through discriminating eating habits, and by promoting self discipline and appetite control. At the same time it preserves our ethnic identity by regulating and limiting the manner in which we connect with the outside world. "Tref" is therefore bad for us; and in this sense so is Wagner. His music causes a physical and spiritual sickness to settle over the 300,000 holocaust survivors in Israel, and over their kindred spirits all around the world. When "Die Walküre" is ingested the soul is sickened. When we sit in the operatic presence of Richard Wagner we fail to separate ourselves from the demonic forces that unleashed the holocaust. All this may have nothing to do with Wagner per se; rather with the way he is being perceived and the symbolism now attached to his music. But the "sickness unto death" that results is the same as if we had eaten "tref."

Rabbi Barry J. Konovitch

PART VI

DIGGING UP THE PAST: BIBLICAL ARCHAEOLOGY

Dr. Yigal Shilo Remembered: Excavator of the City of David

On a July morning in 1978 I struck a pick-axe into the hard-packed earth of what was once ancient Jerusalem as dig supervisor Dr. Yigal Shilo looked on with his characteristic sense of urgency and scientific curiosity. We had the honor of joining the first volunteer group of amateur archaeologists in the history-making attempt to uncover the city of King David. Or should I say we joined Yigal Shilo's "army" of volunteers, since the professor approached the dig project as a general planning an assault on a military objective. Up before the sun was even suspected above the Mount of Olives, we daily staggered bleary-eyed out of our apartment in the newly rebuilt Jewish Quarter of the Old City. The dust of renovation and reconstruction already hung in the air, as if in anticipation of the horde of construction workers that would soon descend upon the area. Through the Dung Gate and down the Silwan road we walked, unaccustomed to the heavy work boots. The water bottles that would sustain us through the long hours in the brutal Jerusalem sun flapped around us, and together with the sound of our tramping feet suggested the approach of an invading army instead of the arrival of two volunteers from America who were hopelessly enamoured with the archaeological search for the past, the Jewish past.

We were late. No matter what time we arrived, we were late. For Professor Shilo it was never soon enough to begin work. Even in those days he seemed to be a man possessed, racing against time, trying to compress a lifetime of work into a few short seasons. Perhaps he had a premonition that for him time was about to run out.

Striding across the grid strings, balancing on the ever-growing baulks, and jumping into freshly opened squares for samples, he seemed everywhere at once.

107

Immediately the stones began to speak of the past glories of Israel's Kings: Herod and Hezekiah, Solomon and David. The potsherds were everywhere, bringing to us a picture of every-day life in the ancient city. A jar handle, an oil lamp neck, a coin, a perfume vial, each fragment speaking more eloquently than the chapters of erudite historians.

The Arab residents of Silwan were curious. The only practical application for holes in the ground was a garbage dump, and in the excavation pits left by former expeditions the basis of the next century's archaeological investigations was already mold-ering away. It was to one such pit, strategically placed, that we turned our attentions one morning. It fell to Aileen to muster a group of Arab boys for the purpose of digging out that all-important garbage dump. Unaccustomed to being ordered about by a woman, and unaccustomed to such demeaning work, progress quickly halted. The water breaks turned into siestas, and siestas turned into mini-vacations. Nonplussed, Aileen took up the shovel and set about digging. Not wishing to be outdone, and therefore embarrassed by a woman, the crew was soon back at work.

By mid-day the sun discouraged any further demonstration of energy expenditure. We retreated to the shade to wash pottery, examine the day's finds, and listen to Professor Shilo offer hypothesis after brilliant hypothesis. He directed our attention to the archaeological evidence: Here were the pick marks of Hezekiah's tunnel engineers, there was the villa of Solomon's wife. Everywhere the evidence of ancient Jerusalem appeared, reiterating a Jewish presence in this city that was some 3,000 years old.

In the first few weeks of the dig a huge glacis-like structure began to emerge on the slope of the now infamous "Area G," quickly dubbed the "monster" by Yigal Shilo. He challenged his visiting colleagues to help him identify it. Several seasons passed before we came to understand that the "monster" was the foundation structure of King David's royal citadel, one of the most exciting discoveries of the archaeological century. It was in this same "Area G" that the dig faced its most difficult problem, not from the uneasy Arab residents, not from the sharply sloping terrain, not from the precariously located excavation pits, not from the burning sun or physical effort. Not even from the United Nations commissions. Rather the problems came from Jewish brothers who appeared one day in their black coats and hats angrily gesticulating into the sand piles of "Area G," claiming that a medieval Jewish cemetery had been disturbed. They demanded that work cease immediately. Bits and pieces of bone were examined by the Rabbinical authorities including the Chief Rabbi himself. The expert testimonies of the scientists, both medical and paleontological, were hastily bulldozed aside as the "Haredi" (ultra orthodox) community sought to flex their political muscle. Forgotten was the fact that the entire Kidron Valley was used as a burial area at one time or another in Jewish History, respecting the Biblical injunction not to bury the dead in the precincts of the Davidic city. Gravesites were probably located all around what is today modern Jerusalem, including Meah She'arim if one might be allowed to excavate there.

But the intelligentsia mobilized and contained the "black-hatted horde." Yigal Yadin, Major Teddy Kollek and a host of academic and political leaders appealed for the exercise of reason and restraint. The information uncovered by the excavators of the City of David would be of great interest to both the secular and religious communities, as daily life of Jews in the Iron Age crystallized out of the ancient detritus.

A compromise was readied. Dig "Area G" was reduced, and the work went forward. But Yigal Shilo had incurred the wrath of the fanatics. In an aboriginal corner of Meah She'arim Professor Shilo was cursed for his efforts to illuminate the historical darkness surrounding much of the early monarchy in Israel.

Several years ago he came to lecture at Barry University in Miami, sponsored by the Judaic Studies Department. Following his presentation on the City of David excavations, he asked for questions. Of course everyone wanted to know about the controversy surrounding "Area G." In exasperation he pointed to me and exclaimed, "There is one of my volunteers who happens to be a Rabbi. He is better suited to answer your questions."

Professor Shilo was not a theologian; he was an archaeologist. Professor Shilo was not a politician; he was a historian. He dealt in scientific facts that were painstakingly drawn from the holy soil of Jerusalem, not in the abstractions born of the grotesque union of politics and religion. Professor Shilo was proud of adding a few pages to the historical record of our people. Surely he realized that he too would now be counted among the "gibborim," the heroes of Israel.

Eight years after its inception, the "dig" concluded. By that time my entire family had been conscripted for work, sorting fragments, washing pottery, passing "guffas" (rubber baskets) filled with dirt, and of course the ubiquitous trowelling and shoveling. As the wheelbarrows emptied their last loads on the dump, and the tools were stacked neatly in the shed, we paused to drink a "Le Chayim," a toast "to life." Grimy, sweaty and tired, we considered the years of back-breaking effort. We had transformed the historical landscape forever, adding flesh to ancient skeletons, and breathing life into Ezekiel's "Dry Bones." Jewish history had taken a giant step forward, propelled by the intellectual and physical force of Yigal Shilo and the people he inspired.

Soon after the close of the dig he was stricken with cancer. For two years this mighty ex-paratrooper waged his final battle against an implacable enemy. Only in the fight could there be victory, for the outcome was brutally clear. He fought until his fiftieth birthday, and then fell "sword in hand."

Those who cursed at the enlightenment he brought to the Jewish people will answer to the Creator of all men. But we will always remember him as a genuine hero in life as well as in death. He was much too young to die, but he leaves behind "one hundred and twenty years" of achievement.

"Shilo's soldiers" around the world surely paused in silent tribute when word reached them of his passing. Our thoughts turn to his offices at Terra Sancta where hundreds of artifacts crowd the shelves and boxes of records line the walls as a living tribute to him. His work will undoubtedly be completed by his students. The final excavation report and summary will serve as his epitaph. All of us who now "own" a piece of the Ophel Ridge by dint of our investment of energy and sweat, who "visited" with our Judean ancestors in their homes and shops, who became intimates of the royal household and whose knowledge of Jewish history has been transformed will never forget Yigal Shilo.

Whenever I visit the City of David Archaeological Garden I will continue to look for the tall, powerful man in the straw cowboy hat whose commanding presence ever urges me on to uncover one more clue to our precious past. His name is written on every ashlar and lintel . . . and he is recorded forever on the stele of our hearts, and the bullae of our minds.

Anointing Oil of the Israelite Kings

The recent discovery of a 2000-year-old jug of balsam oil as reported in the news media presents historical as well as organic identification problems. The ancient persimmon plant, now extinct, is referred to in the Talmud (Tractates Yoma 38b; Berachot 43a). From these references it is clear that the persimmon, called "Afarsimon," was used as a perfume oil and a spice.

However, the ingredients of the Biblical anointing oil (Exodus 30: 22–25), which was used to anoint the High Priest Aaron, his sons, the appurtenances of the Tabernacle, and the Israelite kings, did not contain persimmon. It was composed of olive oil mixed with various other spices.

Biblical descriptions of the anointing of the first Israelite kings, Saul, David and Solomon, refer only to the use of a "vial" or "horn" of oil, the same anointing oil whose ingredients are mentioned in Exodus (I Samuel 10:1; I Samuel 16:13); I Kings 1:39, Rashi Commentary on I Kings 1:39).

Maimonides indicates that only Kings who were direct descendants of David were anointed with the "Biblical oil"; all others were annointed with persimmon oil (Laws of Kings 1:10).

Furthermore, Rabbi Adin Steinsaltz in his modern edition of the Talmud explains in a gloss that persimmon oil is to be equated with balsam, in accordance with Israel botanists (Tractate Berachot 43a). This famous balsam (The "Balm of Gilead") was also an ingredient of the Temple incense known as "Tzori" (Tractate Keritot 6a).

Thus the persimmon oil not only figured in a lucrative perfume industry during the Roman occupation of Judea, but was in constant demand by the priestly incense manufacturers for the Holy Temple. And it served to politically differentiate between royalty directly descended from the House of David and all others.

"The Judges of the Gates"
Letter to Dr. Avraham Biran,
and Answer

Professor Avraham Biran
Hebrew Union College
Nelson Glueck School of Archaeology
Jerusalem, Israel

Dear Professor Biran:

It was a pleasure seeing you again in Jerusalem last month.

With reference to your research on the ancient use of the interior city gate at Tel-Dan and the plaza area in front of it as a meeting place for judges or elders of the city and/or the king:

Consider the prayer "Yekum Purkan" which is recited on Shabbat as a prelude to the Musaf service and whose Aramaic text would indicate that it was composed in the Babylonian exile, although it was not included in the siddurim of Amram Gaon and Saadia Gaon, but comes to us from the text of the French Machzor Vitry:

U-l'daynei di baba

I believe the correct translation would be "the judges of the gates."

It would appear that well into the Babylonian period, the city judges continued to meet in an area or building near or in the gate as in the ancient Israelite period; or they were known by the title "judges of the gate" which merely recalled the ancient practice and came to be used in the Babylonian period as a title whose use conjured up a chain of judicial tradition reaching back to the period of the Judges.

113

Before I proceed with further research I would like to have your opinion.

Best wishes for a bright Chanukah.

Yours truly,

Rabbi Barry J. Konovitch

Rabbi Barry J. Konovitch,
2045 N.E. 186th Drive,
North Miami Beach, FL 33179
U.S.A.

18 December 1991

Dear Barry,

Many thanks for your good letter of November 27. I very much appreciate your interest in our research.

You are right, of course, in calling attention to the mention of the 'judges at the gate' in "Yekum Purkan." In future lectures I shall refer to this and bring Geulah l'olam by crediting you with this reference. As for the date of the composition of the "Yekum Purkan" it was probably composed during the Gaonic period in Babylon. I doubt if the reference to the 'judges at the gate' can serve as evidence for an actual custom or practice so long after the Babylonian exile of 587 BCE. Rather it may be considered as reflecting the survival of a custom of bygone days.

With best wishes and warmest regards, also to your family,

Sincerely,
A. Biran

Modern Idols

A man who hadn't opened his Tephillin bag since his Bar-Mitzvah, suddenly started putting them on daily. A Jewish cult figure had convinced him that he would be protected from sickness. A woman began taking apart every Mezuza in her house. A Jewish cult figure had convinced her that a mistake in the parchment could lead to a burglary.

I put on Tephillin; and I carry major medical health insurance. I have proper Mezuzot on my doorposts; and I have a computerized alarm system. Tephillin is not a Jewish cure for cancer and Mezuza is not a Jewish burglar alarm. Anyone who tries to convince you to the contrary is a modern idol worshipper leading you to paganism.

In the Jewish tradition we do not put our faith in objects; not even Tephillin, not even the Mezuza, not even the Torah. We don't consider our ritual objects as good luck pieces or instruments to ward off the "evil eye." Prayer is not a magical incantation, and a Rabbi is not a magician. Not even a long beard and a big black hat can hide the fact that we are all human, all G-d's creations, all equal, all deserving of G-d's attention, but all mortal.

We put on Tephillin to remind ourselves to use our G-d-given talents and energies to find a cure for diseases that afflict us; to encourage our talented young people to pursue careers in medical research, to donate our money for cancer research; to prompt our political leaders to appropriate less money for weapons of destruction and more money for the war against disease. Tephillin cannot cure cancer, but we can. Tephillin is a motivator, a trigger that redirects our thought processes each morning, a reminder to us of what humanity still needs to accomplish.

We put a Mezuza on our door to remind ourselves that our home is supposed to be a place of refuge from the tensions of the working world; a place of harmony and peace; a corner of sanity in an insane world; a place of holiness (Kedusha) in an obscene environment. Mezuza reminds us that there is a lot more to a home than architecture, engineering systems and landscaping. The Torah actually refers to a home as a "minia-ture temple" (Mikdash Me'at), a place where G-d's presence can be felt.

G-d doesn't live in the Mezuza, as he doesn't live in the ark of the Torah or even in the synagogue. He lives in every heart where there is honour, respect and love.

And Mezuza reminds us to protect ourselves not only spiritually, but physically. Mezuza is not a force-field against the guns and knives of criminals. Burglars are deterred by a good alarm system, or a loaded 45. Each time you walk into your house and kiss the mezuza it should remind you of the holy obligation to protect yourself and your family.

In my collection of archaeological artifacts I have a small Canaanite figure. It was an idol worshipped by the original inhabitants of Jerusalem more than three thousand years ago. But for me it is only an interesting statue. I don't believe it will bring me good luck, make a million dollars, or cure my aches and pains.

On my door there is an Agam Mezuza, a gift from a friend. I don't worship it; for if I did, it would become an idol like my Canaanite figure. I kiss it as a reminder to try to make my home life a little bit better each day; to spend more time with my children, to express my appreciation to my wife more often.

The Mezuza and Tephillin are holy objects. But their holiness resides not inside their little boxes but in the hearts and minds of those who use them properly.

The "Tower of David"

High on Jerusalem's old city walls stands the "Tower of David." It points its slender finger at G-d in heaven reminding Him that the Messiah is too slow in coming. Tall and straight, sitting astride the formidable fortifications guarding the Jaffa Gate, the tower is certainly an appropriate representation of the power of David, the first Jewish rule of Jerusalem.

Yet the Tower, and for that matter the wall complex, has nothing to do with David. Archaeologists have long ago determined that the walls were built by the Ottomans under Suleiman the Magnificent, some 2,500 years after David. And the Tower is, in reality, the minaret of a mosque from whence the muezzin proclaimed the ascendancy of Islam. David, interred in his city to the south on the Ophel ridge, would not rest easy had he known.

Perhaps it is just as well that we know the truth about the Tower. Because David chose a different structure to represent his life. According to his own writing (in the book of Psalms) he refers to the "Succah," or desert hut, as affording him the greatest protection from his enemies. Not a tower, not a palace, but a flimsy booth of branches and sticks.

The "Succah" represented David's life on the run, commanding a guerrilla army trying to elude the forces of King Saul, hiding in the natural terrain on the edge of the desert, away from prying eyes. It afforded him natural camouflage and constant mobility.

In the South Hebron Hills, or at the oasis of Ein Gedi, David's "mighty men" adapted to their natural surroundings. They could venture forth, undetected, to harass Saul's armies. A stronghold was too confining for such tactics, a fixed position too limiting.

And yet, a person who forsakes a palace for a Succah hut must have more than strategy in mind. Open to the elements,

totally unprotected, and exposed to attack, the Succah reminded David that in the end only faith in the power of G-d
would save him. It was this beautiful, personal, trusting relationship that David had with his Creator that is represented by
the Succah.

In later years David finally built his tower. It was atop his
palace in the new Jewish capital, Jerusalem. And judging from
its recently excavated foundation it was a mighty fortress. Such
are the trappings of kingship expected from a powerful poten-
tate. Yet David never forgot the "old days," trying to stay alive
and consolidate his power. It was always clear to him that
without G-d's help, his swords and spears would not carry the
day.

Some 3,000 years after David, our world also seems to be
represented by the "Tower"; the long fingers of intercontinen-
tal missiles that "tower" over our civilization, threatening to
erase all traces of our existence. Those ICBM fingers point
accusingly at us all; We have allowed it to happen.

Perhaps we would be better represented by the Succah, a
symbol of an open, uncomplicated, trusting time when leaders
put their faith in G-d, and respected His creations.

Is it unrealistic to envision a day when the silos in New
Mexico and Novosibirsk will stand empty, overgrown with
Succa brush, silent testimony to the triumph of man's innate
intelligence, and the expression of his Divine image?

The First Overpass in History

When King Herod renovated and reconstructed the Holy Temple in Jerusalem he assured his place in history. The new "Bet Hamikdash" was the largest and most impressive shrine in the ancient world, overshadowing anything that the Greeks or the Romans had ever conceived. The City of Jerusalem became a focus of pilgrimage and tourism, thereby enriching the local merchants, and ultimately the King's treasury.

Herod was sensitive to the concept of city planning. With the tremendous increase in pilgrims streaming toward the temple, he had to maintain the flow of traffic while at the same time preserving the residential nature of the city. Quality of life through careful urban planning was one of Herod's main concerns.

The busiest street in Jerusalem was the shopping arcade located at the foot of the Temple Mount and abutting the upper city suburbs which housed the patrician Jews of the period. Each pilgrimage holiday brought tens of thousands of tourists crossing the main shopping thoroughfare to gain access to the Temple area above. By routing them up and over the shopping arcade Herod relieved a great deal of the congestion.

The overpass carried the pilgrims up to the Royal Portico, an area facing the Temple across a magnificent esplanade. In the portico offices, money could be exchanged, valuables stored and sacrifices purchased. At one point even the "Sanhedrin" held court in the portico. It is interesting to note that many Jews took offense at these commercial institutions in close proximity to the temple. (One is reminded of Jesus' rage against the money changers as described in the new Testament.)

Visitors today may view the remains of this spectacular arch as they walk through the Dung Gate and toward the Western Wall plaza. Protruding out of the southern corner of the West-

ern Wall is the so-called Robinson's arch, the point at which
Herod's overpass originally entered the temple compound.
One would have expected the Romans to destroy the overpass
when they burned the Temple. But the overpass was so skill-
fully built, and its stone blocks were so huge and precisely
placed, that it was too difficult to dislodge it. Ironically it was
the Jews themselves who destroyed the overpass during the
civil war that raged between the "hawks" and the "doves" of
the late Second Temple period. What the Romans couldn't do,
the Jews did to themselves.

The overpass was covered by the debris of history until its
remains were rediscovered by Meir Ben-Dov and Benjamin
Mazar and their team during the famous Temple Mount dig
that started in 1968, a year after the Israeli army liberated the
old city of Jerusalem.

To this day the term "Herodian" is synonomous with brilliant
architecture and monumental construction. Since the discovery
of the overpass and its system of approach roads we can now
add "traffic control expert" and "urban planner" to King
Herod's many accomplishments. His talents could certainly be
used today in a Jerusalem that is often characterized by snarled
traffic, congested streets, noise and air pollution, and the
resultant notorious Israeli tempers.

The Archeologist

A visit to Jerusalem affords us the opportunity to renew our ties with the ancient tradition. A walk through the Jaffa Gate and into the Old City is more than just a stroll past curious buildings and picturesque people; it is an entrée into the heart and soul of Jewish history, a passage into a time machine that instantaneously transports the wayfarer back to the era of kings and prophets.

Our visits to the holiest of cities usually coincides with Tisha B'Av, the day set aside to commenorate the destruction of the temples, and the end of Jewish political independence. It is traditional on this day to walk around the ancient city walls in order to be reminded of the past glories of the city and to pray for the rebuilding of the Temple. Doctor Zev Vilnay, distinguished professor of history and archeology, and author of the most complete guides to Israel (in Hebrew), leads this yearly circumvallation of the walls, and I have had the opportunity to be with him on a number of these processions. This year Aileen and I brought along the youngest devotee of Israeli archeology ever seen on the hike around the walls. Jonathan, equipped with sun hat, and hiking shoes, waited with us at the assembly point for the people to congregate. We chatted with Professor Vilnay, reminiscing about previous years and listening to his observations about the plans for a reconstructed Jerusalem.

Soon the signal was given, Jonathan was slipped into his pack on his "Abba's" back, and off we went, climbing over boulders, up hills, and across dusty valleys to gain the best vantage points from whence to view the city. Passing beneath the Tower of David, the Professor began to comment on David's founding of Jerusalem, but the first and last word out of his mouth was "David." Jonathan, who is a great admirer of the second king of Israel, and who knows most of David's history by heart, began to recite the story rather loudly. A few minutes later, with the applause of the whole party echoing across the Valley of Hinom, the good professor explained that he had nothing more to add, and we were off again, this time with Jonathan *and* the Professor leading the group.

Pausing outside the Dung Gate Professor Vilnay explained that the area is a veritable treasure trove of ancient artefacts, as the residents of ancient Jerusalem would expel all their discarded household items out through this particular gate. He was busily explaining that archeologists are actually garbage collectors, when all of a sudden a column of dust started to rise from the midst of the group. Jonathan, having grown a bit restless, had wandered away from the rest of us, and upon hearing that we were standing on a spot where archeologists were fond of digging, he promptly dug in.

Coughing and gagging, the group moved on, but not before Jonathan had uncovered a few artifacts. His bits and pieces, having been rejected by the Jerusalem Museum of Archeology, now "decorate" his room.

A few hours later, Professor Vilnay, with his able assistant Jonathan, brought the group full circle to our starting point, all of us tremendously impressed by their erudition and enthusiasm for their subject. Posing for a picture with Jonathan, he turned and said to him in Hebrew, "May you continue to join the circumvallation of the walls for the next fifty (50) years, and may I, Zev Vilnay, live to be your guide." A more beautiful wish for life and health I have never heard, and I only wish that the good Lord concurs.

PART VII

SPORTS: A TICKET TO THE MAINSTREAM

Spring Training, 1973

By now most of you know that I am a confirmed Yankee fan. In the last several years I have been wondering why, but nonetheless I manage to stick with it. Last year at the end of the season I caught myself saying, "Wait until next year." But I immediately bit my tongue. I wouldn't want to bring the "tzooris" of the old Brooklyn Dodgers into Yankee Stadium.

Spring training began last week as it does every year. But things are just not the same. The Bronx isn't the same. Yankee Stadium isn't the same. I suspect that both are going to be sold to the Indians, or to whomever it was that we stole the Bronx from. Very little seems to be the same. I asked one of our Hebrew school kids if he thought Bobby Murcer would be as good as Mickey Mantle, and he responded with, "Who's Mickey Mantle?"

But the entire baseball world doesn't seem to be the same. Those great superhuman heros with bats seem to have disappeared. And I didn't really understand just how much things had changed until I chanced to hear a sports broadcast concerning one of the recent Yankee trades. No, Willie Mays wasn't traded back to the Giants. No, Ron Bloomberg wasn't traded to the A's. Mike Kekich traded with Fritz Peterson. They traded their families. When I first heard of it, it didn't register. Just what did it mean? I soon learned that it meant that Mike Kekich was now living with Fritz Peterson's family and Fritz Peterson was living with Mike Kekich's family. And they called a press conference to make it official in case someone hadn't heard.

Sportscaster, after editor, after clergyman began to denounce the dastardly deed. How dare they. Heroes and idols to millions of youngsters, and not so young youngsters. What a terrible example. A "shanda" as we might say. One of my colleagues wrote a scathing letter to the Yankee front office threatening immediate heavenly retaliation. Probably a definite last place finish.

But who are we to moralize about the lives of two baseball players? Since when did we become holier than thou? This kind of thing, or things quite similar, go on every day in every community in America. Why should Mike Kekich and Fritz Peterson be expected to act any differently?

I'll tell you why, because baseball players are not supposed to be human. They are supposed to be above this kind of thing. They are supposed to be endowed with those superhuman qualities that will guarantee them a place in the heart of every sports fan.

But just one moment. Who endowed them with these super-human qualities? We did. That's who. We endowed them with those superhuman qualities. We insisted that they be models of behavior for our young people. We insisted. But they re-fused. As I have said: Baseball players are only people, with a will of their own. Most of them refuse to accept the image that we create for them. Most of them will do what they want and when they want, society be damned.

They are paid to hit home runs, not to attain sainthood. It is we the public who seem to equate home runs with sainthood. And it is we who are mistaken and therefore terribly disap-pointed. Since when is Mike Kekich the guardian of the public morality? Since when is Fritz Peterson the spiritual leader of New York City? They are only men, very average men at that, and the average man was never known to be a paragon of virtue. A high batting average or a low ERA has nothing whatsoever to do with a man's ethical conduct.

I am reminded of so many of our Biblical heroes, who often turned out to be just human. And they *were* expected to be models of conduct. Moses, David, Abraham. Each one had their human failings in spite of themselves. And they *were* trying to conduct their lives in an ethical manner, to be the model for all the people.

Samson comes to the rescue of the Hebrew people. His parents dedicate him to the service of the Lord. His mighty strength will be used to defeat the efforts of the Philistines. And what does he do. He goes off to cavort with the Philistine women. This is a model of behavior? This is the superman? Obviously physical prowess has little to do with spiritual refinement.

And obviously baseball players have little to do with being moral models. If they choose to be, then all the more power to them. I can still remember the likes of Lou Gehrig, the man of baseball. Courageous, indomitable, on the field and off the field. A beautiful model for the youth of America. When he died there wasn't a dry eye in the Bronx.

Surely you and I would like every baseball player to be Lou Gehrig, but it just isn't in their contract. We are just going to have to realize that what we demand of ourselves is the maximum that we can even think of demanding from our ball players and even that is usually too much. After all, how can we legislate private morality for the American League? The American government is constantly under fire for trying to do just that to us.

All the same, wouldn't it be nice to sit at Yankee Stadium and remind your kids that Bobby Murcer eats his spinach and Ron Bloomberg helps old ladies across the street, and Willie Mays is always respectful to his parents. But it just isn't necessarily so. Even the National Israeli Soccer team was recently charged with illegal conduct, and they are Jewish!

Our idols are smashed. Our boyhood dreams were all built on air. Everything has changed. Too bad.

Competing Against Myself

The alarm clock wasn't needed. Thunder and lightning flashes had me up well in advance of 5:30 A.M. In one hour I was due to check in at Bayfront Park, the site of the annual Bud Light Triathlon in Miami. After being "magic-marked" with a body number I would find my assigned spot in the transition area. With my bike hung in its appropriate place I would spend the next hour trying to control my anxiety, all the while wondering how I would fare through the one mile swim, twenty-five mile bike race, and six mile run. All this in one crazy morning.

But it was raining. Hard.

Soon the rest of my "support crew" was up and preparing to go. Gathered were helmet, biking shoes, running shoes, swim cap, numbered jersey, clipboard, stopwatch, race instructions, and three quarts of gatorade in the latest "yellow flavor." Realizing that the weather was not cooperating, to say the least, they looked at me to give the signal: On to the race or back to bed. What would it be?

For the last few months I had dutifully logged the requisite miles around the condominium oval, across the community center pool and through the park. Bike, swim, run. I could tell the day of the week by what venue I was practicing in. Specific muscle and joint pains charted my weekly workout. If it was knee joints it must be run day; if it was "quads" it must be bike day; if it was shoulders it must be swim day. I vacillated between ice pack and heating pad. I even swallowed an occasional asprin.

At age forty-six I still looked forward to breaking the three hour barrier. It would place me in the top three of the 60–65 age group category. But no matter, it would be my personal best, and not bad for a person whose major daily physical activity consists of jumping brain neurons across their synapses in record time. Mental activity needs physical involvement

128

as its counterpoint; one refreshes the other. Some of my best ideas have occurred to me on the 18th lap, or during the 20th mile. With all that adrenaline and endorphin coursing through my blood stream I am as clear as Timothy Leary on an LSD trip. That is, until my forty-six year old body reminds me that I am overextending myself.

I am out to demonstrate that the speed of the aging process can be hauled down from a gallop to a stroll. The twenty year olds are going for the record; I am going against myself. If growing older cannot be eliminated in this life, then at least it can be made comfortable and even pleasurable. To line up with hundreds of athletes of all ages in the dim dawn and prepare to compete head to head for a few hours; to have the audacity to expect to cross the finish line; to develop the confidence and stamina to reduce last year's mark by eight minutes; to be in the select company of the world's finest athletes (if only for a few moments at the starting line); this makes the hard hours of training worthwhile. Waiting for the starting gun, surrounded by all those "speedo" encased, perfectly proportioned bodies, with their muscles tuned and tensed, I feel energized. Youth is contagious.

To be considered as part of this fellowship imparts a special honor and unique feeling of accomplishment. Most important, it announces that the latest skirmish against the forces of aging has been won. The war will never be won; but I am successfully harassing and slowing the enemy advance.

My friends want to know "what I expect to prove." The nature of the question betrays an inability to ever understand my purpose. I merely smile and accept the inevitable amateur psychoanalysis that relegates me to the limbo of permanent, pathetic adolescence, while my more mature friends gather at the local bagel bar for a weekly infusion of low density lipids.

The rain is falling faster and harder. I recall what it is like to take a wet corner at twenty miles per hour with less than an inch of rubber between you and disaster. Am I expected to swim through a lightning storm? Do I expect it of myself? Am I about to cross the fine line between fitness and obsession?

I give the signal. Back to bed. We will rest to fight another day.

Monday morning's paper headlines the race: "Several hundred triathletes brave thunder and lightning, heavy rains and high winds to compete." I spend the rest of the week wondering.

Jews and the American Pastime

You probably realize that it is extremely hard to unite all of our Jews into one solid group to undertake one joint project. No matter how important the cause, one segment of our population always dissents. Where you have three Jews, you have three synagogues, and some say even four synagogues.

But I am glad to report that recently we all finally got together for one purpose. And that was, to watch the 1972 World Series. I have yet to meet one Jew who didn't follow it in one manner or another.

There was a time, and it wasn't so long ago, that we Jews didn't need any T.V. or radio broadcasts to remind us that the World Series was upon us. If you were the average 3 times a year Jew, and you found yourself in the Synagogue, then you knew it was World Series time. To this day, there are strange stories that still persist about the yearly coincidence of the World Series and the High Holy days. We still hear how the scores were announced in some congregations in order to keep the people in the synagogue.

And when New York was treated to what Mel Allen calls a subway series, Rabbis would begin to tear their hair out. One game in the Bronx, and the next game in Brooklyn or in Manhattan. From Yankee Stadium to Ebbets Field or the Polo Grounds. And in between all this pandemonium, Rosh Hashana would have to take place. Well, it was quite a battle as to what would take precedence. Duke Snyder or Al Chet. Willie Mays or Nesaneh Tokef. Joe DiMaggio or Kol Nidre, and I quickly add Le'havdil.

By the way, I once phrased a question to one of my congregants in just the same manner. I was annoyed that the World Series should take precedence in his mind over the synagogue. I asked him straight, "What's more important, Mickey Mantle

131

or Al Chet?" He looked at me for a moment, and very seriously
he asked, "Does Al Chet also play for the Yankees?"

The point of all this is that baseball occupies a great part of
the Jewish consciousness in America. Not that we are the only
sports fanatic Jews in the world. You should attend a soccer
match in the Ramat Gan stadium or the Jewish sports center in
Mexico City and you will see what I mean.

But for us in America, baseball has always been important.

Hank Greenberg used to thrill the kids in his old Bronx
neighborhood. When he was home for the World Series, he
would take time off to bat out flies in one of the empty lots.
And in case you didn't know, Hank Greenberg could hit. As I
recall, about 59 homeruns in one season.

Sid Gordon of the old Boston Braves was another. The Jewish
kids would go wild in the stands when he came up to bat.

And so it went down through the years right up to our own
Mike Epstein and Ron Blomberg of the Yanks. The kids and
even their parents still get a kick out of rooting for their own
boys. After all, the kid who cheered for Sid Gordon is now the
parent whose youngster cheers for Mike Epstein.

I recall that some of the most important arguments that we
ever had as youngsters centered around the alleged Jewishness
of certain players. If the name had a Jewish ring, we always
claimed him as our own. We were very ethnic conscious already
in those days. In our circles of flipping cards and Yankee
Clipper specials, we made more converts for the Jewish people
than all the Rabbis of the Bronx put together. One day we even
investigated the possibility of claiming the great "Dimagg" as
our own. Joseph was no problem, but his last name proved to
be just too much of an obstacle, even for us.

But having Jewish sports heroes was very important to past
generations. A Hank Greenberg meant that Jews were being
accepted into American society. The greenhorns were finding
their way in the new country. We were learning the rules of the
game. And we were beginning to excel.

In the same manner, one can trace the rise of every ethnic
group in America in the last 5 or 6 decades. Sports have always
been an important gateway into American culture for all minorities. In the early stages of ethnic acceptance, sports becomes

the major barometer. Later on will come excellence in the various professional and intellectual spheres. Excellence of a more important and lasting nature. But in the beginning, the fastest way to the American limelight was through the dugout in Yankee Stadium.

We Jews are still sports conscious, but we are no longer obsessed with it. We leave the obsession to the more recent arrivals on the American scene. These minorities who are still struggling to make it in American society, and who are using the time honored method of excellence in sports.

I noted with sadness the passing of Jackie Robinson at 53 years of age. When the Brooklyn Dodgers gathered enough guts to hire him, he made history. The first black to break into modern big league baseball. A hero to his people. An example for all to emulate. The black man could become part of the American scene. Surely it was only a beginning, a symbol in those days, a token as we would call it today, but what a beginning. Only another minority, such as we Jews, could appreciate what it meant.

Today the wheel continues to turn. It becomes quite clear to me in this last World Series that new heroes had arisen for the latest minority to begin the long struggle upwards. Ball players with names that reminded one of San Juan and Caracas and points south, dominated the game. The Spanish-speaking minorities were taking the well-trodden path toward ethnic acceptance. I listened to an interview with one hero of the series and he could hardly communicate in English. Instead he said hello to his mother in his native tongue. But it didn't matter in the slightest. Every fan in America understood him when he came to bat. The sound of the bat against the ball is probably our only international language in America. An American Yiddish if you know what I mean.

And so, baseball has been good to us, as it continues to be good to all American minorities struggling for recognition and acceptance. Thankfully, we have reached the stage where we no longer have to measure our success with batting averages, R.B.I.'s and E.R.A.'s. But we will continue to follow the game. Through it, we will always recall a most important chapter in American Jewish life.

Two on Two

Several weeks before the annual picnic I issued a challenge to my friends: My son and I would take on all comers in a little "two on two." For those who didn't have the opportunity to spend the better part of their boyhood in the playgrounds of the inner city, "two on two" is how we played basketball when a limited number of youngsters were playing "hookey" on a given day. The two players on the winning team stayed on the court until they lost a game or until they dropped from exhaustion.

Each spring, on the first day we could take off our winter coats, we sneaked out of school and headed to the neighborhood playground. For a peanut butter and jelly sandwich and a few cookies, one of our classmates would agree to answer for us at the afternoon roll call. The ritual of "two on two" would be played out between faded yellow lines, a rusting orange post supporting a bent hoop, and a caved-in chain link fence. It was too early in the season for the "Parkey" (the official city park superintendent) to make the necessary repairs. With the snow barely melted, the playground was still chained and locked; the city council was not expecting us for another month. So we climbed whatever was left of the fence, we boosted our lightest classmate up the pole to straighten the hoop, we scratched new lines on the asphalt, and the game began. Under a clear sky and a bracing spring breeze, which would soon be forgotten in the humid weather inversions of the city summer, we flexed our winter-stiffened adolescent muscles. The games would continue several times a week until the principal discovered our absence. His annual appearance behind the chain link fence would signal a visit to school by our parents and the postponement of our games until school was out. But it was this rite of spring that in retrospect underscored the exuberance of our youth. We could play for hours on end until it was too dark to see the hoop. We walked home in the gathering dusk secure in the thought that our energy was boundless; there would always be another spring and another game, and we would always be joined in the brotherhood of sweaty tee-shirts and black "converse" high-tops.

My son is now the seventeen-year-old. He wears sneakers that are surely first cousin to Neil Armstrong's "moon-boots," and expensive enough to supply my old neighborhood friends with sneakers for an entire summer. It takes him fifteen minutes to adjust the laces, and the velcro straps.

"Don't you think we should practice a little before the picnic," he suggests. We agree to spend a few hours at the local community center with some of his friends. Heaven forfend that the "old man" should embarrass him at the picnic.

On the appointed night, his friends slowly gather under the glass backboards, shuffling across the varnished wood court in their high-tech "swooshes and stripes." What was supposed to be a friendly evening of "two on two" suddenly shapes up as a "full court game." To make matters worse they insist on playing until twenty-one baskets, the equivalent of a full quarter with the Miami Heat. I can only hope for a quick loss to save myself from total collapse.

I have one advantage. Seventeen-year-olds have not yet attained their full height. I have a few inches over them and they consider me the "big man." I am assigned to play "down under," Kareem Abdul Jabbar for a night. But I have forgotten what it is like to play against seventeen-year-olds.

A seventeen-year-old is all energy. He never tires. He has legs like springs. He is all elbows and knees. And when you bump into him under the backboards you are the one who will remain sprawled on the floor while nine other players are already in place at the opposite end of the court.

But all is not lost. Without a referee watching I can utilize the old playground techniques honed by countless summers of practice. A hip there, a shoulder here; a feint, an interception, an elbowed rebound and a tap-in.

Guile, intimidation and brute force are the weapons that I bring to bear on youth.

I spend two hours running up and back and by the end of

the evening I am wondering how I will get up for work the next day. My knees pads are down around my ankles and perspiration is dripping off my nose. I slump on the bench. I am exhausted, but somehow elated.

Racing across those shining floor boards I have succeeded in temporarily reversing time. Under the basket there is always another game to play. The ball thumps, the sweat glistens, the adrenaline flows, and I am still surrounded by seventeen-year-olds. Their youth is contagious, and for a short while it is possible to ignore if not negate the ravages of age.

Three days later, on the morning of the picnic, my knees ache and my back is sore. My son is confident that we will acquit ourselves well in "two on two," and I am flattered. But I have already won the contest.

When to Advance; When to Retreat

Two mountaineers set off to climb the Matterhorn in the vicinity of Zermatt, Switzerland, probably because (in the words of Sir Edmund Hillary, conqueror of Everest) "it was there." It presented a physical and spiritual challenge: physical because a great ideal of power and stamina would be required; and spiritual because more than strong legs are necessary to reach the summit. The mountain is also a test of sheer determination. When the heart pounds furiously, and the lungs can't get enough air and each step upwards becomes a struggle, only determination propels the feet.

At ten thousand feet with the peak in view, the brilliant alpine sunlight suddenly retreated in the face of angrily pursuing storm clouds. The warmth of the afternoon quickly faded to a memory as the wind whipped at every inch of exposed skin. Lacking wind clothing the cold soon sapped their already exhausted supply of energy. Breathing became a struggle and each step a major effort. But the peak was already in view, not more than 200 feet above.

The thought that they would not come this way again propelled them to the outer limits of their endurance. But will is only an adjunct of endurance, not a substitute. Slowly the realization set in that the mountain had triumphed; it was time to retreat. Tomorrow there would be other mountains to conquer.

Each of us has a mountain to climb; it is the journey of our lives. At the top we expect to find the fulfillment of our dreams; perhaps success, or peace of mind or whatever our goals happen to be. But we occasionally come to a point on the mountain where progress is denied us. The path is too steep, too dangerous, too enervating. We are out of breath and drained of energy. Yet we persist in struggling upward even in the face of overwhelming odds, convinced that eventually we

137

will conquer the mountain. But even the most seasoned moun-
taineer knows that occasionally he has to retreat and try a
different path.

Persistence has to be tempered with intelligence. There is
more than one way to climb a mountain. A strategic retreat in
the face of overwhelming odds is not a failure; it is merely an
advance in the opposite direction.

Moses once climbed the mountain of Sinai to receive the
Torah. His goal was to bring the word of G-d to the people of
Israel. But he failed; he never reached the summit; the people
ignored him. Down he went, smashing the tablets along the
path. But he tried again. This time he took a different approach, a different path. And the second time he was successful. Persistence and determination are admirable traits. But
persistence without intelligence is mere stubbornness; and
being stubborn is a sure way of destroying ourselves on the
mountain.

PART VIII

THE NEW GENERATION

"Meet Jonathan"

There is a little fellow in our house. He hasn't been there long but he already demands the undivided attention of everyone in earshot. And the little guy has a way of getting it. In the middle of my supper, or at three in the morning, or just as I begin a book, I hear him. Loud and clear. "Pick me up, play with me, pay attention to me." I don't really understand his language yet, but his tone of voice and facial expressions leave no question in my mind. And when he finally has my full attention, he explains to me what living is really all about.

He shows me how fascinating the world around us really is. He insists on examining every item within sight. He turns toward every sound. His senses are awake and tuned to the universe. An electric light, a dog's bark, the sun in the window, a robin singing. He looks in amazement, his eyes wide with wonder. Nothing bores him, everything interests him.

Through him, my own senses are reborn. I see again. I hear again. I come alive to the sights and sounds of the world around us. Why haven't I been looking? Why haven't I been listening?

The little fellow shows me leaves rustling in the wind, white clouds against a blue sky, squirrels in a tree. Everything is beautiful to him. He smiles so easily. He is so easily contented. He knows no fear.

And I smile. Perhaps ruefully. One day, little fellow, you will find out that the world is not all smiles and beauty. The world can be ugly and harsh, and dissonant and fearful. Let me tell you little fellow, that your older brothers are busy removing every last bit of beauty and tranquility left in this world. By the time you grow up there may not be a world worth living in.

But he tells me: "Don't despair. The world is an exciting place. Full of wonderful and beautiful things. Just that you have to notice them. Lie down on your back. Look and listen.

141

Marvel at the Lord's creation. The problem with you is that you are too sophisticated to wonder anymore. If you would pause just once in a while and really take a look, you wouldn't be so downcast. If you cannot see the beauty, then the world is truly dissonant. No wonder you are bent on destroying it.

"It is not the world that is ugly. It is you who are ugly. You, the people who have eyes but do not see, ears but do not hear, hands but do not feel, feet but do not walk."

That's what the little fellow says. And I'm supposed to be teaching him!

By the way. The little fellow's name is Jonathan. And he's so smart because he's my son. I suspect he will have a good deal more to teach me. I'll keep you posted.

Someone New

For the first few days it didn't quite register. "How is your daughter," they would ask, and several seconds would pass before I consciously connected myself with the question. The situation is improving; I have begun to consider pink dresses, white bonnets, and dolls along with the heretofore obligatory baseball paraphernalia.

Our household has changed somewhat: The night is filled with unusual sounds and the sounds are followed by footsteps stumbling through the darkness. I am amazed to discover that the footsteps are often mine. Getting into the car requires a precision operation involving car carriage (top disconnected, bottom folded into the trunk), baby bag, assorted diapers, bottles and teething rings that don't fit in the baby bag, mosquito netting (it is Florida, isn't it?) and other assorted items. The washing machine and dryer seem to be in perpetual motion, ingesting mustard colored crib sheets and spewing forth the original white variety. Filled with Spockean wisdom we have carefully programmed Jonathan for his role as "big brother" (not the CIA variety) and the much vaunted jealousy syndrome has been kept to a minimum. He helps to care for his new sister and is proud of his involvement. The only spark of annoyance flashed from his eyes during our first visit to the pediatrician's office. In his usual authoritative voice he demanded to know why *his* doctor was spending so much time with little sister. The moment soon passed, however, as he quickly admonished our medico to be more careful as he inserted the ear instrument. You can imagine the doctoral response.

Jordanna Ziona is almost a month old now and she has been well integrated into our household; it seems as if she has always been with us. I am more concerned with the future lately. I muse that boys raise themselves, in a way, but not girls. I don't

143

mean to imply that parental guidance and education is inconsequential. Not at all. Just that boys can take care of themselves for the most part; young ladies require a great deal more pampering, protection and persuasion. This may not augur well for women's lib, but it remains a feeling in my bones, as yet unproven.

Being involved in birth must be akin to having lived through the original creation. The feeling that we have must be close to the feeling that the Lord had when he brought Adam and Eve to life. The creation of new life heralds the re-creation of the universe. Each new soul opens wide the door of unlimited potential; each new heartbeat transfuses the world. With each new life walks the promise of Messianic perfection.

Will the potentialities be actualized? Will the promises be kept? As the New Year dawns we fervently pray that they will.

Best wishes for a happy, healthy and meaningful New Year from Aileen, Jonathan, Jordanna and your Rabbi.

First Grade

It was difficult to sleep, even until the appointed alarm clock hour, because he was up and about. The banging of his lunch box against the chair betrayed the fact that it was overloaded with enough provisions to sustain him through several days of drought and famine. It would later pop open at the most inopportune time; just as he was greeted by his peers at the entrance to school.

His face betrayed a certain degree of apprehension as he wrestled with the fact that the world of play was quickly receding into the background. The yard of swings and monkey bars was suddenly superseded by the room with books and pencils; and a freedom bordering on occasional anarchy was quickly harnessed by structure and schedule. He was used to books, but now they had to be read, not memorized. The intricacies of the English language were about to call forth his total powers of concentration and comprehension. The time of testing was upon him and self-doubt was vying with confidence for supremacy of his six year old psyche. We would not know the outcome until 3:00 P.M.

Off he marched with his new bookpack in place, crammed with the entire array of superheroes flitting about his notebooks. They would escort him as he made his way through this unknown territory. The Kipah was jauntily fixed toward the side of his head in the usual manner. But today it would still be sitting there (although mostly covering his ear) because today he would be the rule instead of the exception. Ten children taking the first tentative steps toward the synthesis of Jewish tradition and American culture. Ten children who would undoubtedly form the nucleus for future community leadership. A "minyan" who would be responsible for saving future Sodoms and Gomorrahs.

But these weren't his thoughts. He was wondering about

145

where he would sit; who he would play with; how he would answer those formidable questions that would surely thunder forth from teacherdom. Out of the car he climbed, and after a quick embrace, he disappeared through the door, grimly smiling as he left his babyhood behind.

3:00 P.M. A huge smile bursts into the house announcing success. He recites a litany of new and wonderful things encountered on this momentous day. Work has not displaced play; rather they have blended to allow the learning process to proceed under the best possible conditions. "I'm definitely going back tomorrow," he announces as he runs over his sister on the way to the playroom.

He has stepped onto an escalator from which there is no turning back. Inexorably it will propel him toward a yet unknown destiny. His forward motion suddenly makes us aware of our own movement. He will never stand on the same spot again and neither will we. He is older—and so are we.

Relevant Words About Relevance

In the past few decades most of our established institutions have come under careful scrutiny, especially by our younger people. And with that scrutiny has come the demand for change, for the elimination of that which is found to be morally untenable. The fact that these institutions have been heretofore acceptable means nothing, and indeed should mean nothing to the young idealists. An establishment is created by the people for the benefit of the people, whether that benefit be physical or spiritual. When that establishment no longer serves the needs of the people, and certainly when it seeks to undermine the very well being of the people, it no longer is deserving of continued existence in its original form, and perhaps not even in any form. The truths perpetuated by establishments are relative truths. Relative to, and dependent upon, surrounding conditions. Conditions change. Relative truths change. To demand responsible, meaningful change is not only a right but a responsibility when that change becomes necessary, and with establishments, there eventually comes such a time.

But there is an institution that is an exception to this general rule. That institution is Religion, the Jewish Religion to be exact. Judaism is not an establishment created by the people, only for the people. It does not deal in relative truth or relative needs, but in absolute truths and absolute needs.

In the world of establishments religion stands apart, not subject to the same kind of scrutiny and not subject to the same kind of change. Eventually it is the function of Religion to change us, and not our function to change Religion. This is part and parcel of the definition of Religion.

All that is true, and therefore all that is good can be found within the framework of our Religion, if one has the patience and perseverance to find it out.

But even in the realm of the Religious establishment there is room for change. Change in the sense of what we must emphasize and what we must stress given each new set of environmental conditions. Judaism has the power to address itself to every new problem and to every new concern. Whether it succeeds or not in this most important function, depends on the knowledge and the perseverance of its adherents. Those who do not have the requisite knowledge or perseverance will clamor for change through elimination.

The principles of a government may be eliminated or amended. Men have the power and the responsibility to do so, as they see fit. But the principles of Judaism may only be re-emphasized, and re-directed and re-adapted. Jews have the responsibility to discover those principles and to amend their own lives accordingly.

It is very clear that with the institution of Religion, as well as in any responsible institution, there is no room at all for subjective change, based on convenience, personal preference, or personal feeling. However, every institution, as well as Religion, has to remain sensitive to the needs of the people. Judaism has not only remained sensitive to the needs of the people, but for the most part has been successful in filling those needs, precisely because Judaism contains within its system all the necessary ingredients for doing just that.

We call this ability relevance. Our religion is relevant. It is we who are occasionally irrelevant.

I am often inclined to think that when our younger people question our Religious values, it is not really those values that they are questioning but rather the way their parents have practiced them, or not practiced them. Perhaps our Religious value system is being challenged because we have failed to accept it wholeheartedly into our daily lives. Our youngsters have seen through us. If the Jewish system of values is not good enough to be accepted by the parents then perhaps it isn't good enough to be accepted by the children? Perhaps in effect, our youngsters are judging us and not our Religion?

I for one am glad to find that our younger people are quite vocal when the subject of Religion is broached. It shows that they are bothered by the eternal questions, that they are groping for answers, that they are sensitive to, and aware of the human condition. We should join together often to debate and to discuss, the young with the old. We can all use an occasional shaking up.

But let us not confuse heat with light. The light will come only when we begin to recognize some of the basic truths about our Judaism. And most basic of all is the fact that we do not judge Judaism according to our relative standards; but rather we judge ourselves according to Judaism's absolute standards.

If we do not measure up, it is folly to break the measuring stick.

The Jewish Guru

Last spring I returned to San Francisco. Several years had passed since I had been to the only other city in the United States that could exercise a strong "come hither" influence over me. The city on the bay does indeed have a magical quality about it, and the thousands of young people that gravitate toward it are eloquent testimony to its tremendous attraction. It is a beautiful city, (when you can see it through the fog) with the kind of beauty that seems to inspire quiet thought and contemplation. It surrounds one with a sense of serenity, with a feeling of being at peace with the world. Its particular charm quickly sets a harried easterner at ease, and so many of them have elected to remain.

For awhile, until the newspapers reported it out of existence, San Francisco was the center of the hippie community. This was before the movement was glamorized, popularized and vulgarized to death. The remnants are somewhat in evidence in the "Hashbury," and being curious I spent an afternoon there. To my great surprise I learned that a new center had opened its doors, called the "House of Prayer and Meditation." Its director was none other than Shlomo Carlebach, of Hebrew folk song fame, all decked out in the requisite beads and hippie paraphernalia. It had finally come, a hippie synagogue, complete with folk rock services, yoga meditation sessions, and sure enough a real, live, Jewish, Guru-rabbi.

After the initial ear to ear grin began to wear off I was more than ever convinced of something that I had suspected for a long while. In their rejection of the material world, and in their quest for a better one, our young people are finding the answer in the mystical-religious experience. There are religious communes across the United States dedicated to the improvement of the lives of their members, and committed to aiding all of mankind. Their "religions" seem to have a common element:

150

"A faith in man's potential for producing a transcendent creative energy once he is freed from cultural inhibitions or "hang ups." There is a strong distrust of purely rational thinking and a fascination with the mystical.

One member of a commune expressed the idea that God is within us all, and that man only has to choose to overcome his material side and experience this force that brings people together. Each of us is a fraction of the Infinite.

All of these profound and noble ideas are found within the framework of our Jewish religion. And as I walked the streets of Haight-Ashbury, I thought to myself what a fantastic religious revival would come about if our Jewish young people could understand this very point. If only they would realize that the key to the Good Life lies within their very own tradition; that the blueprint for an "Aquarian age" can be found right in the pages of the Five Books of Moses.

If only we could get this across to them.

You and Your Young Adult

I have just spent what must be termed a youth oriented week. As a matter of fact, I am now supersaturated with young ideas and feelings after spending long hours in earnest discussion with some of the brightest youngsters of our community. From all over the country our college students returned home, and with them came the very latest concerns of their generation. So too did our high school students give vent to their innermost grievances and doubts as they sat around the table in face-to-face debate.

One young man surprised me with this question: "Rabbi, why do you talk to us?" As you can imagine, I was a bit taken aback by the question and I immediately assured him that I wasn't receiving a fat lecturer's fee for my efforts. But the question indicated a certain misgiving, a certain mistrust of my intentions. Was I there merely to play the same old record, to take him and his colleagues to task, to admonish them in loco parentis? Or was I there to listen, to sympathize, to understand, and perhaps to help.

I explained to that young man that it was important for me to know how he and his peers thought and felt. Often parents come to me and ask me to explain the behavior and the attitudes of their children. I am usually in a better position to explain young people to their parents than the young people are. In a way I am able to bridge the communications gap that exists between parents and their children.

The young man quickly realized that I was a good friend to have and he asked that I continue to plead his case, and so I shall:

As parents we have the choice of telling our children what to do, or training them to make their own decisions. We can help them to create patterns of living so they can face their dilemmas on their own, so that they won't have to keep running to their

152

parents for help. Or we can exercise an over strict discipline on them and dictate their every thought and action.

I suggest we give them the freedom to develop their own selves. The freedom to cultivate self-confidence, independence, resoluteness, which will always serve them in good stead.

It may be a simple and quick process for a parent to demand that his son become a doctor or a lawyer. This will solve his vocational problems for the moment. But it won't make him happy: It won't make him a good doctor or a dedicated lawyer. In the long run, a young person will be happy only if he learns for himself what his life's work should be. A parent who provides his child with the tools for choice is by far to be preferred over the parent who does the choosing for him. A person whose parents helped him to develop inner strength will be far healthier and stronger than the one who continually leans on the strength of others.

And finally when the die is cast, when the choice is made, a parent must learn to accept it graciously. There is nothing to regret if the parental responsibilities have been carried out in a conscientious and enlightened manner. The time must come when you must look upon your children not only as part of your family but as part of the greater family of man, equal partners in society.

Bridget Loves Bernie

The names of Adam and Eve are familiar to everyone. The first record of a human marriage. A very unusual marriage no doubt. The bride is chosen not for the groom, but from the groom. From his rib to be exact. The only witnesses are the birds and animals. The Chupah is the sky above, and the aisle is the grass below. The Lord himself is asked to perform the ceremony, and oh yes, the affair is catered by Eden, and flowers are gratis. The Lord, in his remarks to them, must have commented that it was a most auspicious occasion. And indeed it was.

It marked the beginning of the human race. Civilization had come to the world. And marriage was here to stay.

Today many people might take issue with that statement. According to some, marriage is as much of a fantasy as the longitude and latitude of the Garden of Eden. Such people are still in the minority, however. It should be noted that their ranks are thinned each year as they in turn succumb to marriage. A conservative is, after all, a radical who gets married.

But if marriage is still very much with us, marriage styles surely have changed.

The latest fad is to be married in a tremendous meadow under the trees. The bride wears a garland of flowers, no one wears shoes and the wedding dinner is an al fresco picnic on the grass. Actually this is nothing new. Adam and Eve used the very same hall.

But what is new are the bride and groom. Who they are and what they think.

Today the bride's name is Bridget and the groom's name is Bernie. The bride is Christian, and the groom is Jewish. This fact makes as much difference as the fact that the groom has dark hair and the bride light hair. In other words, it doesn't make the slightest difference. Bridget loves Bernie. That's all that matters. Or so it seems.

We Jews have been fighting tooth and nail to maintain our identity since the day Abraham sent Eliezer to find a nice Jewish girl for Isaac. We have occasionally joked about the idea, but down deep in our hearts we always knew it was no joke. It was quite serious. Deadly serious. The marriage aisle was the entrance to Jewish identity. If you approached with a Jewish partner, you entered into the ranks of the Jewish people. If you came with a shiksa or a shagetz, as the case might be, the door slammed in your face. You cut yourself off from your people. You disappeared. You became a non-entity. Your chapter of Jewish history was closed, even before it was written. You were mourned by your people. You were dead to our tradition.

Then tradition mattered. Then Jewish identity was of paramount importance. Then the responsibilities of 4,000 years of Jewish history were taken seriously. But now Bridget loves Bernie, and nothing else matters.

Nothing else matters and no one really seems to care. Not even some Rabbis.

Saturday evening on Simchat Torah we were occupied in the Synagogue. We danced and sang with the Torah. Because we rejoiced in the knowledge that we had cast our lot with Jewish history. We joined our voices with those of our brothers and sisters around the world. We were a united people. United in our love for our tradition. United in our determination to maintain our identity at all costs. And for some of us, particularly in Russia, the cost may even be the ultimate one.

It was on this evening, so I am told, that Bridget and Bernie solved their first great problem. That of an identity.

After all, they too wish to know who they are. When you add one and one you get two. One Jew and one Jew equal two Jews (at least at the beginning). One Catholic and one Catholic equals two Catholics. One Seventh Day Adventist and one Seventh Day Adventist equal two Seventh Day Adventists (or maybe one 14th Day Adventist).

But what do you get with one Jew and one Gentile. You get spoiled chicken soup. You get a mish mash. You get plenty of tzoris. You get a heartache. You invoke the law of diminishing returns. In short, you get another statistic. Another serious loss to the Jewish people. And the mathematics is such that we can little afford it. One Jew and one Gentile is not addition. Not for us. For us it is clearly a case of subtraction.

You also get something brand new. You get an ecumenical ceremony. At least that is what Bridget and Bernie decided to get, along with far too many of their contemporaries. For those who are not cognoscenti in such matters, an ecumenical ceremony requires the participation and blessings of both a Rabbi and a Priest. It amounts to adding stale kreplach to spoiled soup. All you get is an even bigger stomach ache.

I cannot answer for the church, but I can answer for my own colleagues. Those of us who are of a traditional mind, would not have anything to do with such a catastrophe. Those of us who have any feeling at all for Jewish tradition, those of us who have any idea at all of what Jewish existence is all about, would turn away in disgust. How can we expect to preserve even a remnant, a "Shearit Haplayta," of Jewish people if we give our blessings, our tacit consent to intermarriage?

Those who insist on playing up to the current fads are hastening the destruction of their people. These rogue Rabbis are as deadly to the Jewish people as the Christian missionaries. The result is exactly the same.

But we are all responsible for our fate. When it comes to Jewish marriage, there must not be any compromise. In this case, there can be no heart transplant. Because the foreign organ will be rejected by the Jewish body eventually, and the patient will die. All the parts must be authentically Jewish. It is the only way to survive.

The basic lesson of Jewishness must be carefully taught to all of our people. Youngsters, oldsters, parents, children, teachers and Rabbis. Tradition must conquer fashion; principle must conquer pleasure.

Bridget loves Bernie. But who loves the Jewish people? The Lord? I can assure you He won't if we won't.

A Rabbi's Son

He sits in the first row of the synagogue; I sat in the last row. He seems to enjoy his position as "the Rabbi's son," wearing it as a badge of his importance. I, on the other hand, was always embarrassed by the unencouraged attention. Each time I entered the synagogue I felt all eyes swivel and lock onto target, scrutinizing the color of my tie and the length of my cuffs. In an effort to be as unobtrusive as possible I would hurry to the seat nearest the door. The horror of even considering a walk down the main aisle to the front of the sanctuary kept me on a track to the back seat. Invariably the only notice I attracted was that of my father, whose Rabbinic seat on the platform gave him an unobstructed view of everyone's coming and going. My coming was usually late, and my going was early; another strategy calculated to encounter as few congregants as possible. Heaven forfend that I might be questioned about the intricacies of Jewish law or an abstruse point in Talmud, or horror of horrors, asked to lead the service. The several hundred members of the congregation would certainly criticize every vowel and every trope of my rendition.

My father, the Rabbi, was delighted when I did manage to accompany him to the synagogue at the prescribed hour. We would review the Biblical portion of the week, looking for new insights into the ancient text. Those moments of intellectual creativity would often form the basis of my father's future sermons.

For some strange and perverse reasons I relished offering my unsolicited critique of those weekly Rabbinic discourses. My criticism was not confined to textual interpretation, but carried over into voice modulation, gesticulations, and even the rake of the skullcap and fold of the prayer shawl. Perhaps it was a way of expressing my dissatisfaction not with the Rabbi, but with the enforced role of the "Rabbi's son."

I never advanced beyond the last row in the synagogue until the day I assumed the position of Rabbi in my own synagogue. And then I was suddenly catapulted into the very first seat of the synagogue platform. From the first moment of arrival at the service to the last, all eyes were riveted upon me; when I stood they stood, when I sat they sat, when I spoke they listened. Occasionally I yearn for the anonymity of the last row.

But my son sits in the first row. He waits expectantly to be called to lead the service. And to anyone who cares to listen he holds forth on the inner meaning of the prophetic reading, or the apparent reconciliation of Jewish law with modern life. He has just passed the age of Bar Mitzvah but already wears the title of "Rabbi's son" with grace and aplomb. He too offers a critique on every sermon. Poetic justice. But his words are meant to solicit an invitation into the select company of a four generation Rabbinical dynasty; not to declare his independence of it. And I contemplate his unmistakable movement toward the Rabbinate with mixed emotions.

I sit wrapped in my robe of office, a gift from my father who conferred it upon me the day I was ordained. Its black folds embrace me as my father's arms, generating a feeling of comfort and security. But occasionally I still wrestle with those arms. As Jacob wrestling with the angel of his destiny, I too struggle with the intellectual and physical demands of my position, burdened by the expectations of my distinguished forebears.

My son's brow is smooth. It is not yet furrowed by the concerns of adulthood. He doesn't struggle with angels; he walks with them. He accept his place in the chain of tradition. He sits in the first row.

I Sang With My Father

Last Shabbat I had the pleasure of sitting with my father on the Bima of Temple Beth Shmuel.

It has been quite a long time since the two of us have had the possibility of joining together in prayer and study on the Shabbat, precisely because we are both practicing Rabbis, each committed to our own congregations. Spending the Shabbat with my parents brought home to me one of the most tragic failures that so many of us have. Namely, the relatively small amount of interest and time that we give to the people who are closest and dearest to us.

We seem to have time for everyone, except those who need our time the most. We are busy establishing a successful relationship with everyone except those who need our relationship the most. And we measure our success in terms of everyone except those who could really stand for our true success.

Years ago I saw a rather beautiful and moving film about the relationship between father and son, entitled, "I Never Sang for My Father." It was direct and artfully simple in its statement of emotional issues. Melvin Douglas was the father unable to communicate, perhaps unable to feel any love for his son. Gene Hackman, as the son, was in turn oppressed by his lifelong inability to please the old man, to shake free of him and grow to full stature.

How many of us are responsible for creating this sort of generation gap between ourselves and our fathers, between ourselves and our children? How many of us have not been able to cultivate the art of communication in our own households? Perhaps we forgot that it requires a substantial investment of the one commodity that is most precious to us. Time.

We have time for everything and everyone except our own.

How tragic it is that only after time runs out for our familial

159

relationships, do we suddenly realize how little time we have invested. When it is too late to enjoy the company of our dear ones, we begin to yearn for their presence.

The High Holiday season is a good time for each of us to take stock of the beautiful relationships that are afforded us in our lives. If we take them for granted, if we do not cultivate them, if we fail to value them, we shall have forfeited a great deal of what life has to offer, and one day, when it is too late, we shall bitterly regret our failure.

Last Shabbat I sang with my father. And we added a few more notes to that beautiful song of family togetherness. In the New Year of 5750 may all of you learn to sing that song, in harmony with all those who are dear to you.

Day School Education Should be Free of Charge

The number of students in day schools across is miniscule relative to the school-age population of Jewish children.

We are justifiably proud of the proliferation of day schools and the increased financial support that has been forthcoming from Federation. But a viable Jewish future in America requires universal day school education. This should be our primary weapon in the fight against an assimilation rate of over 50 percent.

However, budgetary requirements demand higher and higher tuition; teachers and principals must be paid properly. But higher tuitions continue to limit the number of children attending, not only because there are many who genuinely can't afford it, but because there are even more who refuse to assign it top priority. When the choice comes down to a new car or a vacation as opposed to tuition for children, the day school education loses.

The only alternative, as I see it, is to change our entire approach. We can no longer be satisfied that such a small percentage of children attend day schools; it works against us. We must recognize that the only hope for a viable Jewish future lies in "universal" Jewish day school education.

I would propose that day school education be made available to every Jewish child, "free of charge." As there is really no "free lunch," I suggest that the money be raised by a "universal" education tax on the entire Jewish community. In the same way that our federal and state tax dollars support public education, our Jewish tax dollars would suppot Jewish education. This would place the responsibility for education on the entire community, where, Talmudically, it belongs.

161

The mechanism for collection and enforcement needs to be worked out, but Jewish communities past and present have such collection mechanisms, witness the Syrian Jewish community in Panama where you can't participate in any religious ritual (from cradle to grave) without financial commitment dictated by the Rabbinic leaders. This concept can be modified and adapted in America if we cared to understand that we are in a crisis. The mechanism of Federation has only been somewhat successful; it needs to be adapted and modified. In the process we may find that there is a limit to our resources and that the "pie" needs to be recut.

Traditional beneficiaries of our money may have to be reduced and even eliminated. But at this moment in American Jewish history, there is no greater priority begging for our support than Jewish day school education. Without an intelligent, committed future generation, there will be no American Jewish community of any consequence, and consequently, there will be no strong support for a strong Israel.

PART IX

BLACKS, JEWS AND OTHER MINORITIES

The Crown Heights Riots: A Sermon

A Jew is expected to be tolerant of all people, especially minorities.

Kee gerim heyitem b'eretz Mitzrayim

"Remember you were once a persecuted minority in Egypt."

1. Therefore I can understand the problems of black people in America, especially in neighborhoods such as Crown Heights, and Bedford-Styvesant. I understand what happens to a society when the family unit breaks apart, when there is no father, when the respect for authority is lost. I understand what it means to drop out of high school at 16 with no job skills, when the most you can expect from life is a minimum wage position at MacDonalds. I understand what it means to live in dirty tenement houses, with leaking plumbing, giant rats and non-existent repairs. I understand the frustration and rage that builds up in people when they recognize the futility and meaningless, and helplessness of their lives. I understand all this, I feel for these people, I expect the city and federal government to do something about it. G-d knows we are able to do something when we want to, when we recognize that we are in a crisis. How many billions of dollars did we spent to save our Persian Gulf oil supply? How many lives did Americans sacrifice so that the Kuwaiti sheiks could return to their million dollar palaces, their 100,000 dollar Rolls Royces and their oldtime despotic rule; so that Saddam Hussein could continue to play hide and seek with his nuclear stockpile and make fools of us.

If the American government would choose to see the inner cities as a battle ground that is just as dangerous as the deserts of the Persian Gulf, then it would send in enough men and money to solve the problems. It would be much harder than

165

bombing an electricity complex, and it would take a lot longer than 100 days, but it can be done. We have the resources to do it. We have the teachers, and the professors, and the drug counselors, and the day care managers, and the doctors, and the carpenters and the plumbers and the electricians and the social workers, and the surplus food, and the vocational teachers and the money. But as yet we have chosen not to do anything. To ignore the problems. I say we have the money because this kind of program is a lot cheaper than the costs for welfare, food stamps, emergency hospital aid, unwanted pregnancy, drug abuse, alcohol abuse, increased police protection, etc.

2. Having said all this, now I say to you that all this is no excuse for violence. When Jewish people lived under the very same physical hardships they never rioted in the streets. They never murdered.

When black teenagers loot stores on Kingston Avenue that's called grand larceny, that's called assault. When black teenagers pull a Jew from his car and stab him to death, that's called murder. I'm not interested in the economic or psychological or sociological reasons for their problems. There is never an acceptable excuse for murder. No one is going to tell me that the young blacks were out protesting the accidental death of a youngster by breaking into a Korean-owned sports store and running away with high priced sneakers and shoes. It took them 3 hours to break the iron gate across the store. The police just stood and watched them.

3. Who encouraged those black youngsters to commit murder, premeditated murder, as a proper response to the accidental killing of a child by an out of control car? Their leaders. That is the level of black community leadership in Brooklyn today. A reverend, a man of G-d, and a lawyer, and a doctor encouraging their people to act like animals; suggesting that they solve their problems by going on a rampage through their neighborhood; by attacking the police, by threatening physical harm to the mayor (himself a black man), by murdering a Jew.

Yes, I know; they didn't call for the murder of a Jew. But did you hear one of them condemn the murder? Did you hear the reverend Al Sharpton get up in his church and say that murder is a terrible sin? That the murderers should be brought to justice immediately? That there is a clear and distinct differentiation between accidental death and premeditated murder?

4. The correspondent for the New York Times went out into the street to interview the blacks who participated in the riot. Listen to what they said:

"I helped flip over a police car. It made me feel like I scored a point."

"You want to see how strong the black man is."

"Police are a symbol of repressive and hostile white society. I'm sorry, I just don't like white people." "The guards in jail treated me badly."

"We're black; when we see this we get mad." "We're against the police."

Twelve-to-fourteen-year-olds bragged about throwing rocks and bottles. "It made me feel strong because we were with a lot of black people."

"It was fun throwing bottles on the cops."

On Martin Luther King: "I don't admire him; he let blacks get beat up."

The disturbance gave them something to do. Nothing to lose by rioting. "Boys trying to act like men."

5. The black complaint heard over and over is:

"The Jews get preferential treatment: closing streets for Sabbath and extra police protection for the Rebbe." This bothers the blacks.

The Hasidim are highly organized around their religion. They respect authority, of their leaders. They have tightly knit family units. They live according to a strict value system. In short they live as "menschen." They are everything that the blacks are not. They are everything that the black community would like to be.

And from a financial point of view the Lubavitcher are supported by an international network of fundraising. Financial support comes in from every country in the world.

And Crown Heights is one of the very few remaining integrated neighborhoods. Instead of running away, the Hasidim remained, because it was the decree of the Rebbe. They have stabilized property values. They have improved the neighbor-hood.

6. So what is really the problem? In one word, envy. The blacks are envious of what these people have done with their lives and their community. They are jealous and frustrated that they can't do the same. And the result of jealousy and frustration is the violence we have witnessed.

7. Some of the Hasidim called it a pogrom. For people who witnessed the pogroms in Europe it looked frighteningly famil-iar. Heil Hitler. Looking for mezuzas to stone. But we live in 1992 America, not 1939 Germany. And we have every expecta-tion that our government will protect its citizens, not join in harming them.

I would have expected Mayor Dinkins to call out the National Guard. Why should the police stand aside when people run loose in the streets, looting and smashing and finally murder-ing.

8. Maybe it's time for the Rebbe to speak out. With all due respect, this is a time of crisis for the Lubavitcher Hasidim in Crown Heights. In Jewish law it is called *et la'asot*, a critical time for constructive action. Maybe the Rebbe will decide that it's time to leave Crown Heights. That he can no longer endanger the lives of his Hasidim. Maybe he will decide that it's time to make aliya to Israel and to wait for the Messiah there. Or maybe he will decide to stay and to fight for their rights, their property, and their safety.

But whatever the Hasidim decide it will be in their own good time, in their own way. No one is going to threaten them. No one is going to push them around. No Jew is going to be treated like "hefker" again, without rights, with no protection.

9. I would call upon the blacks to focus all their energy toward moving into American society instead of away from it. I realize how hard it is for them. But they are wrong to reject white society just because it is white. Just as we are wrong to reject black society just becuase of their blackness. And it doesn't help to be called Afro-Americans. That only separates blacks even more. Do we call ourselves Jewish-Americans?

Do Chinese call themselves Chinese-Americans? Do Colom-bians call themselves Colombian-Americans? Our purpose in becoming citizens of America was to remove the hyphen. So why are blacks the only hyphenated citizens, Afro-Americans? It is indicative of the black identity confusion. It is one of the factors that prevents them from becoming an integral part of American society.

Instead of doing some serious soul searching (heshbon ha-nefesh) the black community takes the easy way out by fixing the blame on everybody but themselves. And the Jews, this time the Lubavitcher Hasidim, are the convenient scapegoats. But our history of being designated the scapegoat is long past. Never again will we willingly place our heads on anyone's chopping block.

It is time for the black community to grow up. To stop blaming their problems on everyone and everything but themselves. It is time for them to take responsibility upon themselves, and to take responsibility away from their irresponsible leadership. Ironically, they have the most to learn and to gain from their Hasidic neighbors. If only they would allow themselves to move beyond envy and hatred, to tolerance and admiration.

Resegregating the University

The recent Lindsay victory in the New York mayoralty race can be viewed as a voter repudiation of any appeal, overt or covert, to racist feeling. The majority of our citizens refused to rally behind the flag of those who implied that "the blacks are getting everything." New Yorkers continue to resist being swept along in a white backlash. They still believe that in the long run their patience, consideration, and understanding, even in the face of strong bigoted opinion, will result in a finer community for all.

In these difficult days of hatred and extremism, it is very hard to remain a true liberal. It is difficult, if almost impossible, to extend help to others when we ourselves are often in need of that same help. Although the improvement of black rights and opportunities will eventually enhance the rights and privileges of us all, the immediate results seem to impress most people as "borrowing from Peter to pay Paul." However, those of our citizens who can visualize the future are willing to bear some discomfort in the present.

But several days ago something occurred in Poughkeepsie, New York, that can only serve to severely damage liberal sentiment, and escalate the backlash activity.

Thirty-five black students occupied the Main Hall of Vassar College. These young women reported that they would not end their occupation of the hall until the college was legally committed to granting all their demands. These demands included a black studies program with a degree to be granted upon completion of the required course of study. We may disagree with the tactics used against the college, and we should oppose the idea that force is an acceptable means of changing a university's policies. But we can understand the need for black studies in the same way we approve of Oriental studies or Italian studies. Any student who has the desire

170

should be able to explore that area of human knowledge that draws his interest. And if his own identity is clarified and strengthened in the process, then by all means.

But the students also included the demand for *separate* living quarters for all black students.

Now those students attend Vassar because the college administration has realized the necessity for an integrated university society. It was a long time in coming but it came. The college officials have gone out of their way to include black students in the enrollment. All barriers were removed in order to include those young women, who otherwise, because of monetary or scholastic difficulties, could not have attended Vassar. All this to insure a balance of college students, to end forever a segregated university community.

And now the same people who fought for so long to be able to attend a Vassar College, to break the terrible policy of segregated education, have turned around and demand their own policy of segregation. They wish to live, eat, sleep and study only with blacks. They wish to be segregated from the white student community.

If this is so, then why do they wish to attend Vassar? Why can't they enroll in an all Negro college if they wish to be separated from everyone else?

I do not think that Vassar College, like New York City, like the world can tolerate segregation any longer; certainly on the part of white society, and just as certainly on the part of the black society.

If we are going to live together in harmony and accord, then we can do without any demands that begin, end with, or include the term separate.

Letter to Justice Marshall
April 12, 1991

Justice Thurgood Marshall
Supreme Court of the United States
Washington, D.C.

Dear Justice Marshall:

On April 8 and 9, I had the pleasure of viewing a television docudrama that presented the story of Brown vs. the Board of Education, Topeka, Kansas, a Supreme Court case that effectively cracked the "separate but equal" educational system. Although Sydney Poitier was the star, you played the leading role, along with your colleagues Jack Greenberg et al., lawyers of the NAACP in the early 1950's.

I was so moved by this episode in American jurisprudence and civil rights, that I felt obliged to write to you for reminding me of this benchmark episode that I had long ago filed in the back of my mind. To say that you were magnificent in your struggle is to understate the situation. You were courageous, wise, determined and inspired; and even these words don't do justice to your achievements.

For several days I have pondered the state of race relations in America, motivated by this television production, and I have come away deeply saddened. The great promises of the 50's and 60's have turned to the disappointments of subsequent decades. I am ashamed of the fact that race relations seems to have deteriorated, especially in the urban areas of our country. I walk the streets and instinctively fear and distrust a man of another skin color who crosses my path. I must constantly remind myself that generalizations from the individual to the community fan the fires of prejudice, that no group should be judged by the actions of the individual; or better yet no group should be judged, period.

Why have we lost trust in one another? Why do we resent and even hate one another? What happened to the American dream that you and I and so many good people once envisioned and worked for? Where are those people who are so proud to recall their marches for equality with Dr. King et al. but have gone into "retirement" since those heady days?

I am not interested in theological and philosophical answers to these questions, which are actually rhetorical; rather I seek a renewed political effort aimed at the practical and realistic, not the theoretical.

Certainly you have a right to sit back and feel that you have written one of the most significant pages of 20th century history, and no one would dare criticize you for that. But I feel that we are slipping backwards. America seems to be sliding toward a cataclysmic explosion of the races; the evidence is all around us and need not be the subject of lengthy dissertations. Walk along any street, any blighted neighborhood, in any city and you will find immediate and compelling evidence.

To whom shall we turn if not to the Thurgood Marshalls and Jack Greenbergs of our generation. Can we bring together "the mighty men," the men of good will, who can, by virtue of their strength of character, wisdom and sheer "guts," redirect our national conscience?

Perhaps I am dreaming, to use the overworked civil rights slogan. But you may wish to join me in this dream; and if we enlist enough dreamers then the vision may turn into reality.

It would be my distinct honor to hear from you, and to benefit from your comments.

With highest regard,

Rabbi Barry J. Konovitch
President, Rabbinical
Association of Greater Miami

Black Jews, White Jews

Once again the State of Israel has demonstrated its *raison d'etre*. Swooping out of the clouds, the Jewish eagle literally plucked its children from the jaws of death and brought them home. Another twenty four hours and the Ethiopian Jews would have disappeared in the mass of malnourished and starving peasants, condemned to become part of the statistics of yet another African tragedy.

The tiny, emaciated faces imprinted on our television screens shock us, and haunt our sleep. The satellite uplink brings the dying and the dead right into our living rooms. We turn away as does the rest of the world. With the exception of a few heroic relief agencies the world doesn't really care, not about Africa, not about blacks, not about primitive cultures.

But Israel cares. Only Israel cares. The common denominator of our Jewishness cuts across all boundaries of color, geography and culture. Israel is truly color blind, the only country that can make this claim, and for the second time in the history of the modern State. The Yemenites were rescued from Arabia and fully integrated into Israeli society; and the Ethiopians will surely follow suit, in contrast to the Christians and Muslims who kidnapped the blacks out of Africa, sold them into slavery, and treated them as beasts of burden. This is what Benjamin Netanyahu had in mind when he made his historical statement. Decide for yourself who is treated better: an Ethiopian of the Beta-Israel in Tel-Aviv, or a black American two generations removed from a Georgia plantation living in Liberty City? Rampant racism can be found in Arabia, Western Europe and even in America. But Zionism stands before the world clothed in the dignity of equality. The aberrant United Nations resolution attempting to equate Zionism with racism has once again been proven to be a projection of the situation prevalent in those very nations who voted for it. Look for racism in the

174

streams of Asian refugees who poured out of Iraq and Kuwait and were left to starve in Jordanian border camps; or in the Palestinians executed in Kuwait City for pro-Iraq behavior; or in the Christians being systematically destroyed in Lebanon, or the Kurds ignored for weeks by the West, slaughtered by the Iraqis and left to die by the thousands on the borders of Turkey, Iraq and Iran. In comparison Israel should be invested with sainthood; it is indeed a "light unto the nations."

With a quiet dignity appropriate to descendants of Jewish royalty the Beta-Israel descended onto Israeli soil, realizing their dream of centuries. They have come home; and it is our duty to welcome them and to make their transition into twentieth century Israel as painless as possible. We must ease their way into modern society while at the same time preserving their unique culture. They are a window to our past; a veritable lost treasure of Jewish history waiting to be discovered, studied, analyzed and carefully and lovingly preserved. We look to all elements of Israeli society to clear the way for the Ethiopian Jews; particularly to the Chief Rabbinate to remove any religious impediments and to set the example for the rest of Israeli society to follow. Moses himself married a "Cushite" (Ethiopian) woman, thereby setting a personal example of integrationism and tolerance.

For 2,000 years, since our exile from Jerusalem in the Roman period, we have slowly lightened our skin color from Middle-Eastern brown to Germanic and Nordic white. Surely Abraham from Ur didn't resemble Chaim from Vilna, not in color, and not in culture, not in physiognomy and not in dress. Now the pale European faces which had begun to darken with the proliferation of the Sephardim (Arabic and Spanish Jews) will darken even faster with the integration of the Ethiopians. Slowly but surely we will move a little closer to our brown origins, the Caucasian Soviet Jews notwithstanding.

If there remains an authentic looking Jew in the world then he just deplaned from Addis Ababa. He has already re-written the stereotypical description of the "Jewish look." Just when we thought we knew who we were and where we came from he has come with new information to digest and assimilate.

Most important, he reminds us of the eternity and invincibility of Judaism as a faith, impervious to every vicissitude of history and oblivious to all non-religious distinctions, be they political, racial, or geographic.

Welcome back; welcome home.

PART X

EARTH WATCH: ECOLOGY FOR JEWS

Trees

There is a tremendous maple tree in my back yard. I have always considered it to be an annoyance. During the summer, when I wish to spend a Shabbat afternoon reading in the sun, that tree manages to cover the entire back yard in shade. In the autumn, its myriad leaves begin to fall, into the rain gutters choking off the water flow, onto the back lawn creating endless hours of raking chores, and onto the driveway and sidewalks obscuring them from view much to the consternation of my neighbors and visitors.

In the winter its long, heavy, branches extend well over the roof of my house, and when the wind begins to blow the branches begin to drum on the housetop and on the window panes. Sometimes I am tempted to get up in the middle of the night and open the window. Perhaps if I let the branch in, it will stop tapping on the window.

In the spring, little berry-like growths appear on the tree, and as they begin to fall, my back porch slowly turns from gray to "manischewitz red."

That tree is like some of my acquaintances: Tolerated because it is too difficult to rid myself of them altogether.

But last summer I journeyed to a land without trees. The Sinai Desert is not exactly known for its foliage. Trees do not agree with rock and sand and 5 inches of rain a year.

My feud with the back yard maple was soon forgotten in these bleak, treeless surroundings. Forgotten until one day when I was rather graphically reminded.

The temperature was 110°F in the broiling sun and we were only half way up the steep face of Mt. Sinai. We had begun our climb at four o'clock in the morning in order to outrace the sun. But here it was only nine o'clock and the Sinai sun had already caught up with us.

There was no hiding from the sun. Those hot rays bore down

179

upon our heads and backs. The heat waves danced off the rocks penetrating our boots and parching our throats. And the higher the sun rose the slower we climbed. On that mountain there was just no hiding from the relentless rays.

Just when we were about to decide that our next step would be our last, we spotted what seemed to be a tree on a distant ledge. After ascertaining that it really was a tree and not just a desert mirage we quickly made our way into its shade, collapsing in a heap under its blessed branches. It took the better part of an hour but we were eventually revitalized. With renewed vigor we continued on our way to the summit every mindful of our debt to that tree.

Since that day my attitude towards that maple tree in my backyard has changed. Precisely because I know what it is to be without. Never again will I mutter under my breath when the shade covers my backyard. Never will I entertain ideas of cutting down that tree. As a matter of fact remind me to double my contribution the next time a youngster rings my bell collecting for the Jewish National Fund.

Getting Away From It All

Recently I came across a rather interesting article in the paper. It told of a couple who met in a university class, built a sailboat and began living an idyllic life anchored off Miami in Biscayne Bay. They are never plagued by crab grass. Nor with property taxes. That's right, no property.

According to the wife, they wanted a very simple life. They found urban living too complex at times. Out on the water they can enjoy the quiet, and the really beautiful things, like the sunsets, the birds and the gentle motion of the waves.

Only the wind and a small radio ever break the silence and the nearest neighbors are a long swim away. They don't have a phone or a T.V. Only a small library of books.

"We have found out a lot about ourselves and each other, and we are finding out about the world," said the husband. "It's like looking from the outside at society."

As I read this article it dawned on me that the idea would probably appeal to just about anyone. Who wouldn't want to retreat from the hustle and bustle of everyday living, at least for a little while? Wouldn't it be wonderful to escape from the city and shut out the noise and the smog, and the subways, and the traffic, and the boss's orders, and all the other disturbances that begin to make life just a bit unbearable?

And wouldn't it be so nice to sit in all that quiet and open a book for a change? A really worthwhile book. And do some serous reading and thinking. For a change you could begin to find out what your husband or wife really thinks, what he or she is really about. No phone to interrupt conversations, no newspaper to hide behind, no den to retreat into. Just the two of you, in one small area facing each other squarely, forced to give your relationship a deeper meaning, instead of the usual superficial exchanges that pass for family life today.

Sounds good, doesn't it?—Impossible you say? Well think

again. In a few days we shall celebrate the holiday of Succot, and on these days we are commanded to live in booths, in a succah. The Bible says leave your house, with all its comforrts, with its central heating system, with its plush carpeting, and go live in a one room hut. Bring with you a Chumash and a Siddur. Sit in the Succah and admire the stars shining overhead in the heavens. Stand in awe of nature and the Lord, its Creator. Sit with your family and get to know them again. Sit with yourself and get to know yourself a little better. Shut out the everyday world and enter a new world, a world of the intellect and the spirit. Renew yourself.

How many of us have forgotten the true meaning of Succot and the beauty that it brings. This year "Get away from it all," and "escape from the ordinary." Come back to the Succah.

The Fear of Quiet

The ancient Hebrews were nomads of the wilderness, criss-crossing the Negev and Sinai in search of pasture for their animals. But their need for grazing areas may not have been the only factor that motivated their decidedly anti-urban predilections.

According to the classical Biblical sources, the early Hebrews avoided the cities in order to avoid the negative environmental influences that seemed to be the concomitants of urban life. More precisely, they avoided the centers of pagan worship where the newly emerging and yet fragile Jewish Tradition might be severely tested and perhaps overwhelmed.

The desert offered a pristine environment, uncontaminated by the excesses of civilization, a quiet, undisturbed state of nature where a man could commune with the Divine, without being distracted.

In the desert of the Negev near Gerar, Isaac followed his father's example, developing and refining the concept of mon-otheism, and influencing those he came in contact with.

In the desert of Sinai at Horeb, Moses encountered his destiny as the liberator of his people.

But in the city of Sodom, Abraham's nephew Lot lost his soul and almost his life, caught as he was in the silken web of urban decadence. And in the city of Ur Abraham was in danger of losing his newly defined destiny as a Hebrew; he left for a rural promised land in accordance with Divine dictat.

The nature of modern life is such, that we are rarely afforded the luxury of retreat to splendid isolation. Our urban environment is polluted by the excesses of industrial society; it sickens our bodies and poisons our souls. In our collective fantasy we are drawn to the desert where the horizon is an uninterrupted line in the infinite distance, where ours is the only footprint,

183

and where the sounds are of silence. But alas, it is only a fantasy.

Each morning brings anew a clouded horizon, a stifling atmosphere, and a cacophony that masquerades as the music of modern life. Our senses are bombarded to the point of dullness: "We have eyes but we do not see, we have ears but we do not hear."

But even if we could precipitate out all the irritants and pollutants in our societal situation, I doubt we would. In essence we feel more comfortable with the urban noise than without it.

I passed a young man on the street yesterday who appeared to possess two heads. One proved to be a huge portable radio growing out of his shoulder. I noticed him because he was intent on serenading the entire neighborhood. The music, if one may call such shrieking music, made me wince, as human beings are wont to do when subjected to such tortuous decibels. Instead of passing him by as quickly as possible I turned and confronted him:

"Why do you insist on such loud volume? Turn it down and you will be able to hear just fine."

He conducted a quick experiment and agreed that it wasn't really necessary to blast his radio.

Why did he do it? He couldn't really answer until I suggested that perhaps he had a powerful, unconscious need to be noticed. That he was actually afraid of quiet.

He walked away in thoughtful contemplation under the influence of the lowered decibels.

Are we afraid of quiet? Do we fear to confront our innermost selves? Is the noise cranked out by our society a way of attracting attention?

"Notice me," we say.
"Don't forget me," we plead.

The silent desert may be our fantasy, but in reality it would frighten us to death. We cannot bear to be alone with ourselves, with our own thoughts, in the presence of the Divine.

Save the Forests of Judea

On the narrow back road that leads from the Eilah Valley to Bet Shemesh, it is possible to travel for miles without meeting another car. And when you pass a car it usually has the special license plate designation indicating that the driver is from Arabic Hebron. Four weeks ago, my family and I traveled that road on an inspection tour of the Jerusalem corridor forests. Huge black patches glowered at us from surrounding hills, horrible reminders that the latest manifestation of the *intifada* is the destruction of our trees.

For more than 50 years, Jews from around the world have planted those trees, nickel by nickel, *pushke* and *pushke*. A forest of blue boxes created the forests of Israel. Slowly the dull brown landscape, decimated by the avaricious conquerors of 2,000 years, turned green. The harsh glint of the sun was softened, the birds and animals returned, and our eyes beheld the rebirth of the land. What visitor has not been delighted to gaze upon the carpet of green that spread across the Judean Hills, symbolizing in the most vivid and exquisite manner the return of the people of Israel to its land. Only the true owners of the land would invest so much effort, money and love in reclaiming it and caring for it.

And the Arab claimants to this same piece of land, what have they done? With their petrol bottles and incendiary devices they have made this land black. They have burned the trees and destroyed the landscape. This is the way they have chosen to express their "love of the land." This is the way they have promised to care for "their purported national homeland." If they have been unable or unwilling to coax new life into a long dead landscape, then they refuse to accept the miracle of land rejuvenation symbolized by the forests of the Jewish National Fund. To spite their faces they proceed to cut off their noses, because they have graphically demonstrated to

185

the world that their claim to "Palestine" is false. No true son or daughter of the land, would seek to destroy it. Only a Jewish heart can be broken at the sight of hundreds of smoldering, blackened tree stumps. Only Jewish eyes weep at the acrid smoke rising heavenward, another sacrifice on the long road of our history.

On a sharp bend in the road we came upon a fire that had just broken out. An Arab car sped away bound for Hebron. The Army jeep at the side of the road had spotted them starting the fire. A few radioed words of warning to the checkpoint up the road and they would soon be in custody. But we were left to contain the fire before it spread out of control.

Quickly we joined the several soldiers and settlers who had also chanced upon the scene. With our car mats we frantically beat at the flames. Beating here, stamping there, racing from point to point as the dry brittle grasses continued to flame. Desperately we worked to save the trees. Each time we extinguished one patch, another would flame up unexpectedly. Finally we made one line, 9 people, adults and children, Army regulars and neighborhood settlers, all desperately stamping and beating at the persistent flames.

And it was out. Just the smoldering ground to remind us of the catastrophe we had averted. We stood black faced and smelling from smoke but satisfied.

We have planted many trees in our lifetimes, but never were we called upon to save them. Somewhere in the world is a Jewish family who put their nickels into a *pushke* for years to plant those trees. My family and I saved their trees, for them and for their future generations and for all of us.

And now we call upon you to help save the trees. Turn the black hills to green again. Be responsible for replacing just one tree. Replace it with two trees, or 10 or 500. The trees symbolize our return to our homeland, our determination not to be uprooted ever again. The trees constitute the army of the Jewish people, marching against barrenness and ugliness, conquering the wilderness and securing our historical claim to the land. Send a message to our enemies: Our roots are planted deep in the soil of Israel; no power on earth can uproot us. The trees say so.

Helicopters Over Homestead

Three days A.A. (after Andrew) the army was on the move. From Fort Bragg in the Carolinas troops began arriving at the Opa-Locka Airport. The sound of helicopter blades could be heard across Dade County, lifting the spirits of people who were beginning to think that hurricane relief presented greater logistical problems to Washington than the invasion of Iraq. The desperately needed water and food were unloaded by the ton out of the gaping mouths of giant C-5 transports. But the helicopters were needed to bring the supplies South, directly to the people hit hardest by the disaster.

Every citizen of South Florida felt the obligation to help. My son and I followed the line of cargo planes into the airport and there we were put to work loading supplies onto the helicopters. A Boeing Chinook helicopter can carry a platoon of fully equipped soldiers, or two armed jeeps. When the army designed and built them, they had in mind eastern Europe, or the Middle East. Old men with gruff voices and stars pinned to their stiff shoulders envisioned those helicopters over foreign battle fields. Never in their wildest imagination did they expect that the battlefield would be South Florida and that ground zero would be Homestead.

I have never flown in a helicopter. I have been around them; I have seen them maneuver. In Palmachim Air Base, just south of Tel Aviv, I sat in a huge Sikorsky helicopter that can transport tanks. But until Andrew I never flew in one.

By invitation of the pilot we found ourselves strapped in as the huge blades began to circle overhead and the Chinook vibrated, roared and shook. As we lifted off in formation I learned that our mission was to unload the supplies at several points in the Homestead area. Headphones were clamped over our ears, preventing total deafness and allowing us to listen to communications. We unloaded half our supplies at Tamiami

Airport, or whatever was left of it. Small pickup trucks made their way onto the tarmac between piles of wrecked airplanes and twisted hangar roofing. Red Cross officials were trying to keep order but there was no way to determine priority needs. One enterprising person was stopped with a truck-load of tar paper. He was turned back when it became clear that he was going into the roofing supply business a mile down the road.

We strapped in once again as the helicopter shook itself off the ground and flew south. Sitting in the doorway next to the flight engineer I had a clear view of the area. The pictures I had seen on television did not begin to prepare me for the destruction on the ground. Flying some hundred feet above the ground I could look directly into every livingroom; there were no roofs left. In a few minutes missing roofs gave way to missing buildings. Whole neighborhoods were gone, reduced to splinters of wood and twisted metal. We were in a war zone; the only thing lacking were the machine guns. It appeared as if an enemy airforce had swept in and bombed the entire county. Only the plumes of smoke and the craters were missing.

Our pilot was supposed to pick up a new ground transmission that would guide us to the loading zones. As I listened through the headphones it became apparent that we weren't receiving the expected signals; we circled to no avail. The civilians in the target drop areas were not transmitting to us. An attempt was made to land behind a Publix Supermarket; the area was too confined for our huge blades. A second landing zone was rejected at the last second for fear of stampeding crowds rushing toward us. We eventually had to return to Opa-Locka with half of our supplies aboard. Confusion and disorganization were seriously impeding the relief effort.

We are eternally grateful for the young men and women of the military and the army of volunteers drafted by the civilian emergency organizations. But the weak link in the chain is the interface between the military and the civilian organizations. An army has a general, and a clear chain of command. Everyone knows exactly where to go and what to do. If left alone the military could handle any situation with alacrity and efficiency. Civilians are not trained in the same manner and cannot be expected to handle disasters of such magnitude. Their interaction with the military, although well intended, seems to reduce the efficiency of the operation.

As we wearily headed "home" to Opa-Locka at the end of the day I was mightily depressed from what I had seen. Clearly years would be required to bring some sense of normal life to South Dade. A huge, ongoing, unwavering effort would be required from all of us. But catastrophe is a test of civilization; and I have every expectation that we will pass the test. I was reminded that Rosh Hashana marks the anniversary of G-d's creation of the world. Our annual job is to re-create the world. Only this year our job description has been expanded.

PART XI

FROM HAVANA TO MIAMI: THE CUBAN JEWISH EXPERIENCE

Cuban American Jews Take Pride in a Rich Heritage 30 Years Later

At the stroke of midnight on New Year's Eve at the Cuban Hebrew Congregation the band played the *Star Spangled Banner*, *Hatikva*, and *El Himno Nacional*, the anthem of a free Cuba. Thirty years had passed since Castro took power and the communists precipitated the demise of the once flourishing Jewish community. One by one the Cuban Jewish families took their valises in hand and set out for America, 90 miles away, but a world apart.

Once before their destination had been America, but a xenophobic shift in immigration policies concerning Eastern Europeans brought a community of Polish Jews to Havana instead of New York. This time they left behind successful business operations and comfortable homes, along with a panoply of religious, civic, charitable and social institutions. The keys were left in the doors; they would be back as soon as the political winds shifted, and Cuban society returned to normal.

With little more than letters of credit, their good name and a reputation for industriousness, they rebuilt their lives and their community in Miami. Temple Beth Shmuel is not only our synagogue but it is the hub of a huge wheel whose diameter extends across the two-county area and even across the map from Florida to California to Puerto Rico and to Israel, networking all Cuban Jews.

On the surface we seem like any other congregation of Ashkenazic Jews around the world: we pray from the same book, we sing the same tunes, we observe the same traditions, but listen more carefully and observe more keenly.

Greetings are exchanged in Spanish, Yiddish and English, and a limp handshake will not suffice. Only a backslapping bearhug will do. Such animated greetings are usually reserved for family members, and indeed we are almost all related. A product of some 40 years of inbreeding. A tiny isolated community of Jews on a Caribbean Island could only assure their survival by drawing a spiritual curtain around themselves. Refugees from Poland had only the model of the *Kehila* (European community organization) to follow and it served them well. It allowed them to maintain a strong and proud identity as Jews and as Zionists, impervious for the most part to assimilation. They married within the small circle of Jewish settlers, transforming "landsmen" and *Shifbrueder* into an extended *mishpacha*.

At the same time the Latin culture layered itself over the Yiddish and became the Cuban icing on a distinctly European Jewish cake: "Yosef" in the *patronato* synagogue became "Jose" in the *calle muralla* business district; at the bar-mitzvah reception the *horas* alternated with the *paso doble;* and *gefilte fish* shared the table with *arroz con pollo* and *frijoles negros.*

Even so, we never had an identity crisis. We were educated to understand that we were Jewish by religion, and Cuban by citizenship: one complemented the other. There was no sense of contradiction or confusion about who we were.

And when you observe us now, almost thirty years removed from Cuba, our sense of Jewish identity is very much in evidence—witness the number of our children who attend the Hebrew Day Schools, the number of families who visit Israel and the number of people who contribute financially to the welfare of the Jewish people and the Jewish state.

Our American experience has not diluted us. It has merely added one more layer to the cake—making us the major trilingual and tri-cultural Jewish community in the area. Our grandfathers were called *Menachem,* our fathers are called *Manolo* and we are called *Manny,* but there is still a direct and unbroken Jewish line that now connects four generations. And it is these four generations, sitting together in our *shul,* that constitute our "specialness," our uniqueness.

And here you have our secret: four generations of Cuban Jews who respect their elders, who respect their tradition and whose greatest joy is to stand with each other in the sight of G-d at the most significant moments of their lives.

It is difficult to predict what the future will bring to the Cuban Jewish community. We are beset for the first time with the pressure of an "open society" and life in the "melting pot." As with all American Jewish communities, it will become increasingly difficult to maintain our integrity as Jews, and as Cuban-Jews. The forces of assimilation that regularly decimate a good percentage of our people must be slowed and eventually routed. But it can only be achieved through an aggressive and unrelenting process of Jewish education.

We are demonstratively proud of our Jewishness, sprinkled with the salt of the Eastern European *shtetl* and the pepper of the *comunidad cubana*. And we are proud to be citizens of the United States—a country that took us in and gave us opportunity instead of empty promises; a country to whom we have returned a measure and a half for every measure given to us. We look forward to the next 30 years with an optimism born of the realization that we are the children and grandchildren of "survivors"; those gigantic, near mythological men and women who survived two exiles in one lifetime, but prospered against all odds, whose grand history that spans three cultures and constitutes a microcosm of all Jewish history will soon be written so that future generations may be encouraged and inspired.

The Cuban-Jewish Community

People are often surprised to learn that the Greater Miami area is home to the world's largest community of Cuban Jews.

Approximately 2,000 families came to the United States when Fidel Castro established his Communist regime in Cuba in the early 1960's. This "exodus" from Havana to the Greater Miami area resulted in a significant economic and cultural influence that is still evident in South Florida. There are many business analysts who credit the Cuban immigration of the 1960's with the revitalization of the Miami economy and its establishment as the "gateway" to Latin America.

The Cuban Jews, in the forefront of this economic revitalization, came with literally the shirts on their backs. For many it was the second time in their lives that they had to begin again.

In the early 1920's the first generation left Poland and Eastern Europe in the wake of widespread anti-Semitism and economic deprivation. Without knowing a word of Spanish, unfamiliar with Hispanic custom, and uncomfortable in a tropical climate, they soon adapted. Slowly and carefully, with great hardship and personal sacrifice, they carved a place for themselves in the Cuban society. In the relatively prejudice-free environment of the "simpatico" Cubans, the Jewish community made significant strides, establishing the full panoply of educational, religious, cutural and community institutions. All this was virtually stripped from them by the communist regime, to be re-established in Miami.

The "Ashkenazim" or Jews of European ancestry organized themselves into the "Circulo Cubano Hebreo" which eventually was transformed into Temple Beth Shmuel on Miami Beach. It remains the center of Cuban Jewish life in South Florida, and indeed is headquarters for an international community of people who live in South America, Central America, Puerto Rico, Israel and across the United States.

The "Sepharadim," or Jews of Spanish ancestry, established Temple Moses on Normandy Isle to maintain their unique customs and traditions.

The Cuban Jewish community is now tri-lingual and tri-cultural. The oldest generation speaks Yiddish as their primary language; the Cuban-born generation speaks Spanish as their first language; and the American-born generation speaks primarily English. All, however, are fluent in all three languages and have synthesized the three cultures, European, Spanish and American.

The special flavor of this unique community is evident in their social, religious and cultural lives. Synagogue services are conducted in the traditional Hebrew with English readings, explanations and sermons. Announcements are often made in several languages. Celebrations are marked by a confluence of Spanish, Israeli and American Music, cuisine and dance.

The family unit constitutes the major force in contemporary Jewish-Cuban life, together with a strong commitment to religious tradition. The community is noted for its proud support of the State of Israel and its unabashed appreciation for the blessings and opportunities of American life. Its members are leaders in the business and professional community of South Florida and serve as an example of the accessibility of the American dream for those who are ready to work hard.

As the third and fourth generations take their place in the community, the challenge of pluralistic living remains: How to preserve a unique culture slowly being "homogenized" by the "open" American society. As with all minorities that came before, the melting pot has a way of sterilizing American life by modifying and even eliminating cultural differences. Cuban Jews need to resist the trend by serving as a model that seeks to enrich the fabric of American life by weaving into it those colorful and unique strands of the Judeo-Hispanic heritage. To bleach away those colors in an effort to "blend in" would do a disservice to both American life and Cuban-Jewish life.

The Cuban-Jewish community can serve as a powerful force for creative leadership in Greater Miami. In a demographic area dominated by Jewish and Hispanic populations, the Cuban-Hebrew congregations are the only institutions that combine

both constituencies, thereby serving as a bridge between the
two cultures, as a rallying point for a synergistic union of
energies and as an environment for intelligent integration into
the American mainstream.

The St. Louis and the Haitian Exodus
February 12, 1992

To the Editor
The Miami Herald
One Herald Plaza
Miami, Fl. 33132

Sir:

I have been considering the parallel between the Haitian exodus, 1992, and the Jewish exodus, 1939, for many weeks. Howard Kleinberg (Feb. 11) is to be commended for his forthright article on the local reactions to the ship *St. Louis* as she drifted between Cuba and Miami in search of a safe haven for its 937 Jewish passengers, early victims of the Nazi plan to annihilate the Jewish people. Mr. Kleinberg was a member of my planning committee that commemorated, in international fashion, the 50th anniversary of the sailing of the *St. Louis* in the presence of the survivors and their families. The ensuing worldwide publicity brought the "refugee" story once again to the conscience and consciousness of all people with the hope that fifty years later the human environment has changed for the better.

Fifty years ago, as reported by H. Bond Bliss, a handful of South Florida religious leaders decided to "contribute its tiny share in the moral awakening and rearmament of mankind," even though there was little hope of United States intervention in the *St. Louis* affair. But consider what might have happened if the community en masse had demonstrated and paraded by the tens of thousands; if the American religious establishment had descended on their representatives in Washington; if the entire flotilla of Miami recreational and fishing boats had gone out to the *St. Louis* and escorted her to the Port of Miami in defiance of the United States Coast Guard cutter on duty to prevent anyone from swimming ashore.

None of this came to pass. The *St. Louis* passengers were forcibly returned to Europe; most were murdered by the Nazis as the holocaust spread across Europe.

"Displaying a soul," as Mr. Kleinberg describes South Florida's reaction in 1939, is a good beginning, but it just isn't good enough, not then and not now. Displaying a soul may provide some salvation for our souls, but will not save the lives of the oppressed.

On rare occasions history comes full circle and stands ready to repeat itself. And we get a second chance to redeem ourselves. Is this the time? Is this the place? Are we ready?

Rabbi Barry J. Konovitch

The Fiftieth Anniversary of the St. Louis: *What Really Happened*

The S. S. *St. Louis* departed Hamburg, Germany, on May 13, 1939, with 937 Jewish refugees bound for Havana and the free world. By the time she returned to Europe on June 17, the complicity of the western democracies in the destruction of European Jewry was foretold in the newspaper headlines, government communiques, and confidential conversations of diplomats: no one wanted the Jews.

Many writers have been preoccupied with the affair, and the ghastly details have been amply documented.[1] But 1989 marks 50 years since the *St. Louis* sailed into infamy, and in the intervening decades we have grown to realize the enormity of the tragedy. Everyone must share the blame: the Nazis, who were planning for a Judenrein Europe; the American government, including the president, which refused to interfere in an internal Cuban affair; the Cuban government, which bowed to local anti-Semitic xenophobia; the Havana Jewish community, which fearfully and helplessly watched their brothers and sisters sail away; the America Jewish community, whose lack of organization, political clout and moral courage cowed it into accepting the callous decrees of the State Department; and the Hamburg-Amerika line officials who, in concert with the Nazi Minister of Propaganda, allowed the *St. Louis* passengers to sail for Havana knowing that permission to disembark had been denied.

During the late 1930s and most of the 1940s Cuba was one of the few destinations open to Jews fleeing the Nazis. What prompted the anti-Semitic aberration that closed Cuba to the *St. Louis* refugees? Cuban President Laredo Bru made an offer to Lawrence Berenson, the Harvard-educated lawyer who represented the New York Joint Distribution Committee (JDC), for

disembarking the Jews. Why weren't the negotiations successfully concluded?

Most of the literature published since World War II on the
Holocaust refers to the *St. Louis* affair as a precursor of things
to come. Only the *Voyage of the Damned* and "The *St. Louis*
Tragedy" discuss the incident exclusively and in detail, over
the period of May and June 1939, from Hamburg to Havana
and back to Europe. But Lawrence Berenson's failure to secure
the release of the passengers is not adequately explained. If
business as usual in Cuba, 1939, meant providing the right
politicians with the right amount of money, why wasn't Berenson successful in his mission?

Gellman indicates that after a Cuban offer was made to
accept the refugees, Berenson "felt that he could reduce the
admission price." He had already spoken to "his principals" in
New York suggesting that he could "save them a considerable
amount of money." On the following day, the President [Bru]
spoke with the director of Chase National Bank and explained
that Berenson's attempt to bargain and save some money
ended the discussions.[2]

Thomas and Witts report an announcement by the Cuban
government issued on Tuesday, June 6, 1939, at 6:00 p.m.:

> Agreement was reached two days ago with Senor Berenson to
> land the exiles on the Isle of Pines after he had deposited $500
> in cash per person with a subsidiary guarantee with regard to
> their food and lodging. He was given 48 yours to meet these
> requirements. Yesterday Senor Berenson made an alternative
> proposal offering $443,000 for the *St. Louis* passengers, plus $150
> additional for the refugees on the *Orduna* and *Flandre*, the sum
> to include expenses for food and lodging. The Cuban govern-
> ment could not accept the proposal, and having passed exces-
> sively the time allowed, the government terminates the matter.[3]

But a refusal to negotiate on the part of the Cuban president,
or any Cuban politician for that matter, would have meant a
major financial loss, something they were not likely to choose.
The only question should have been is how high they could
force Berenson to go. Instead, Bru cut off all discussion just
when final negotiations should have started and thereby for-

feited all chances for any monetary benefit. Furthermore, Lawrence Berenson's role in the *St. Louis* affair has never been adequately documented. Nor has his thinking and action been accounted for. How could a man with such vast experience in dealing with Cuba, so well connected politically and so familiar with Havana politics, have failed?

In order to fill in the gaps in the story, and in order to flesh out the picture of Lawrence Berenson in Havana and account for his failure to secure the release of the *St. Louis* passengers, we need to turn to the eyewitnesses, who until now have not given their testimony. They are the members of the Havana community of 1939, mostly Jews, who have intimate knowledge of Lawrence Berenson and the *St. Louis* affair. This article draws extensively on their observations and conclusions gathered from personal interviews.

From the moment he landed in Havana, Lawrence Berenson had no doubt he could successfully negotiate the freedom of the *St. Louis* passengers. His overconfidence would be his downfall. Experience had taught him how to do business in Cuba: the right amount of money in the right pocket would always achieve the desired results.

His brother, Richard, owner of the Miami Jai-Alai Fronton, had been travelling to Cuba since the mid-1930s recruiting players. An enterprising businessman, he took advantage of the anti-Machado revolution and chartered Chalk's Airlines to rescue well-heeled political refugees. He met Fulgencio Batista and recommended that his brother Lawrence handle the military leader's legal affairs. Lawrence Berenson and Fulgencio Batista became close associates, and when this last president of Cuba went into exile following the Castro revolution, Lawrence Berenson accompanied him to Trujillo's Dominican Republic.[4]

Berenson was the JDC's logical choice to negotiate the landing of the *St. Louis* refugees. The Jewish lawyer from New York was the former president of the Cuban Chamber of Commerce in the U.S. He had already used his considerable political connections in Cuba to purchase 1,000 visas to facilitate the exodus of Jews from Germany. Although the Cuban authorities were still lenient regarding refugees from Europe, Berenson wished to comply with the German bureaucratic mentality. An "official" document would satisfy the German authorities and facilitate the exit of Jews from the Third Reich. Berenson's discreet political inquiries led him to contact Manuel Benitez, Director General of Immigration. A clandestine meeting was arranged at Benitez' *finca* ("ranch") in Pinar del Rio. Berenson, accompanied by a few armed members of the Jewish community, delivered $125,000 in cash. Within days the Cuban Embassy in Berlin began issuing visas for the first 1,000 Jews on their waiting list.[5]

Benitez grew wealthy from his trade in visas, and the Jews living in Pinar del Rio referred to his local real estate investments and construction as *reparto judio* ("the Jewish suburb").[6] It soon became apparent to the Cuban political hierarchy that fortunes could be made in the sale of these landing permits. Benitez' refusal to share the wealth was one of the factors that prompted President Bru to issue Decree 937 on May 5, 1939, which terminated the power of the Director of Immigration to issue landing certificates.[7] Henceforth official visas had to be issued with the approval of the secretaries of State and Labor and a bond of $500 filed by every alien.[8] Now Berenson was deprived of his main contact; he would have to approach the president.

Once again he came to Havana with cash in a briefcase. His old friend Batista could have opened the doors for him and eventually for the passengers on the *St. Louis*, but he declined to get involved. It was common knowledge that Batista was the real power in Cuba, but he was sensitive to the growing public opinion against refugees and he chose to do the politic thing by making himself unavailable to Berenson or to anyone pleading the case of the *St. Louis*. President Bru would have to be contacted directly, and Berenson was reminded of the consequences if an attempt to bribe the president of Cuba by an American citizen became public.[9]

American isolationist policies caused by grass-roots xenophobia stemming from fear of economic competition and loss of jobs were mirrored in Cuba in 1939. The anti-Semitic overtones became pronounced as the right-wing media began to beat the drums in Havana, as they had in the United States. The Nazis skilfully orchestrated this anti-Semitic sentiment by infiltrating provocateurs into Cuba to stir up the population through manipulation of the media and to secure Havana as the major transit point for transmitting the information gathered by Nazi spies in the United States to Berlin. Unbeknownst to the passengers aboard the *St. Louis*, the Hamburg-Amerika line was being used for carrying this information.[10]

If Batista wished to avoid involvement in the *St. Louis* affair, how much more so did Bru, who would not last a moment in office if public opinion turned against him. On the other hand, the president was well aware that the eyes of the entire world were on him. A refusal to grant asylum to the *St. Louis* refugees on humanitarian grounds would condemn him forever in the pages of twentieth century history.

A delegation from the Centro Israelita, the local Jewish umbrella organization, went to visit the president. He responded by indicating that money was not the issue; every republic should accept some of the Jews in proportion to their population, and if the United States had declined to accept the Jews, why should Cuba accept them?[11] America's refusal to rescue the Jews of the *St. Louis* underscored by a gunboat sent to keep them away from the Florida coast, was a crucial decision that would shortly be expanded into a policy of official indifference to the fate of European Jews, condemning six million to death.

In June 1939, as the *St. Louis* remained at anchor in Havana harbor, 937 Jews looked wistfully at the Malecon Promenade. They could see and smell Cuban freedom, but they could not touch it. Among the factors working against them was a direct communication from Washington to Havana requesting that the Jews not be given passes to disembark because they would eventually request permission to continue on to the United States.[12] And the United State didn't want them for the same reasons that were disturbing the Cubans.

The Jewish colony in Cuba considered the citizens of the country free of anti-Semitism. If anything, the original Jewish immigrants were referred to as *Polacos* ("Poles"). The anti-Semitic outburst of 1939 that resulted in the rejection of the *St. Louis* Jews was an aberration, for in the 1940s, under the presidency of Batista, Cuba welcomed many thousands of

Jewish refugees. But in June 1939, the fears of the Spanish merchants and manufacturers, who controlled most of the economy, were transmitted through the falange-dominated right-wing press and aggravated by local Nazi cells. The result was tragedy.

Lawrence Berenson failed to grasp the complicated and shifting pressures on the Cuban government. In assuming that it was business as usual, he made a fatal error in judgement. The Joint Distribution Committee was officially on record against the payment of bribes.[13] But they were ready to post a bond of $500 for each passenger to guarantee that they would not become a burden to the Cuban government. Berenson was sure the Cubans "would settle for less," but he was wrong.[14]

On June 2 the *St. Louis* was forced to weigh anchor and leave Havana. If no agreement with the government was forthcoming, she would have to sail for Europe. Two days later, at Sunday noon, Lawrence Berenson was admitted to Bru's country estate. The president requested that $500 per passenger be deposited in the Cuban treasury, that a further bond of $150 per passenger be posted to cover their sustenance at the Isle of Pines barracks or elsewhere, and that all arrangements be concluded in 48 hours.[15] On Monday the president repeated his terms to the press in Havana. Berenson now had a clear and definite offer; had he immediately fulfilled Bru's conditions the Jews of the *St. Louis* would all have been saved.

Instead he chose to play by the old rules of Cuban politics, not realizing that the game had suddenly and dramatically changed just as surely as the players had changed. Benitez was out and so were his conditions for doing business. In addition, the heretofore benign Cuban attitude towards Jewish refugees was gone. Bru was completely in charge, by design, and the fate of the *St. Louis* passengers rested entirely in his hands.[16] He found himself on the horns of a dilemma: if he allowed the Jews to land he would jeopardize his chances of remaining president; if he sent the Jews away his name would be disgraced in the eyes of the world. He desperately sought a way out, and his final offer to Berenson offered a solution. Bru and his advisors shrewdly anticipated an attempt to negotiate any terms they presented. By drawing Berenson into this trap they hoped to put the onus for the failed negotiations on his shoulders. The world would understand that the "magnanimous" Cuban government had offered the Jews a haven, but Lawrence Berenson, representing the JDC and the Jewish people, refused to accept this generous offer.

As soon as Berenson presented a counter offer to Bru, the trap was sprung: the president refused to discuss the matter further, the 48 hours passed, and the ship was forced to sail for Europe. The New York JDC office had suggested that Berenson pay the amount demanded, but he elected to "save them money" and see how inexpensively he could secure a safe harbor for the *St. Louis* passengers.[17] Surely the limited resources of the American Jewish community had to be considered, and surely Berenson approached the negotiations in a strictly businesslike fashion. But in the end, 907 Jews sailed back to Europe, most to their deaths, because Berenson did not agree to the price Cuba placed on their heads. Had he immediately agreed to Bru's conditions, the *St. Louis* would have discharged her passengers at the Havana docks. But Berenson may not have been briefed properly as to the unique and dangerous political conditions that prevailed in Cuba in May, 1939. He was familiar with the facts. He was aware that the affair presented a no-win situation for Cuban politicians, most of whom refused to get involved, but he failed to translate these facts into a successful negotiating strategy. Instead, he relied on his experience, and he failed.

Had the Jewish community in America been as politically powerful, organized and wealthy as it is today, and had the Jewish community in Cuba been as influential as it became in the decade before the Castro revolution, Lawrence Berenson's chances for success would have increased dramatically. An effective Jewish response might have overcome American indifference, Cuban confusion, and German mendacity.[18]

Notes

1. Gordon Thomas and Max Morgan-Witts, *Voyage of the Damned* (New York: 1974); Arthur Morse, *While Six Million Died* (New York: 1968), pp. 270–288; Irwin Gellman, "The *St. Louis* Tragedy," in *American Jewish Historical Quarterly*, 61 (1971), 144–156; Haskel Lookstein, *Were We Our Brothers' Keepers?* (New York: 1985), pp. 81–104; Deborah

Lipstadt, *Beyond Belief: The American Press and the Coming of the Holocaust, 1933–1945* (New York: 1986), pp. 115–120; Rafael Medoff, *The Deafening Silence: American Jewish Leaders and the Holocaust* (New York: 1987), pp. 59–62; Gerald Reitlinger, *The Final Solution: The Attempt to Exterminate the Jews of Europe, 1939–1945* (New York: 1953), p. 23; Martin Gilbert, *The Holocaust: A History of the Jews of Europe During the Second World War* (New York: 1985), p. 80.

2. Gellman, p. 15.

3. *Voyage*, pp. 250–261.

4. Interview with Louis Stanley Berenson, nephew of Lawrence Berenson, Miami Beach, 2 February 1989.

5. Interview with Jose Opatowski, Miami Beach, 7 March 1989.

6. Interview with Aron Yuken, Miami Beach, 11 February 1989.

7. Interview with Manuel Benitez Valdez, Miami Beach, 20 February 1989.

8. *Voyage*, p. 147.

9. Interviews with Zeidel D'Gabriel, Miami Beach, 23 February 1989, and Leizer Ran, 6 April 1989. Each new government required new contacts and new bribes. The *St. Louis* affair caught the attention of a large group of Cuban politicians, each of whom saw a considerable financial opportunity. Each would have to be paid even before the public offer could be negotiated. The stakes continued to rise, the situation became more confused, the amounts of money asked became unrealistic, and time ran out for the *St. Louis* passengers.

10. *Voyage*, p. 32.

11. Interview with Leon Gilfarb, Miami Beach, 17 February 1989.

12. Interviews with Manuel Benitez Valdez and with Yudel Steinberg, 28 February 1989; Malka Majerovicz, 13 March 1989; Ben Volpe, 10 March 1989 and Ariel Remos, 28 March 1989 in Miami Beach. Sender Kaplan recalls that many of the passengers held numbers for visas to the U.S. from the American Embassy, which meant they were registered and would eventually be processed officially. It would therefore seem illogical that Washington would request that the *St. Louis* passengers be denied permission to land in Havana as a "transfer point" to America.

13. Interviews with Herbert Katzki, JDC, New York, 22 March 1989 and Abram J. Dubelman, Miami Beach, 23 February 1989.

14. Gellman, p. 153.

15. *Voyage*, p. 249.

16. Interview with Martin Mayer, Miami Beach, 8 March 1989. Bru's legal argument with Charles Silver over collecting insurance for a burned building purportedly caused bad feelings and has been connected with the anti-Semitic outbursts of 1939.

17. *Voyage*, p. 222.

18. Discussions at the Fiftieth Anniversary Reunion of 27 survivors held at the Cuban Hebrew Congregation, Miami Beach, June 3–4, 1989. Liesl Loeb, daughter of Joseph Joseph, the on-board chairman of the *St. Louis* passengers' committee in 1939, asked "What did you Cubans do for us?" Rabbi Barry Konovitch, responding for the Cuban Jewish community, told of the behind-the-scenes efforts that were made. Loeb answered that had any significant actions been undertaken, her father would have been informed since he was in contact with the JDC representatives in port.

PART XII

NOSTALGIA

No One Is Waving

In a far away place called Rockaway, in a fantasy land called Luna Park was a carousel. Its prancing ponies and rearing stallions with flashing hooves and waving manes still whirl madly through the imagination of my childhood. The music would pound, the horses would fly and the giddy feeling would remain long after my weekly visit.

I would always choose the red horse with the black hooves and the golden bridle. It was on the outermost edge of the carousel, and if I leaned way out I had a chance to grab the golden ring. That prized ring was more than a circle of brass; it symbolized the ability of a young boy to overcome his doubts and fears, and aggressively pursue the coveted prize. With trophy in hand, I would triumphantly wave to "zaide" who nervously waited for me to dismount.

My favorite part of the ride was the wave from "zaide." I had someone to share my triumphs with. Someone who took price in my accomplishments, someone who recognized the significance of the capture of the ring. His wave confirmed my victory. It signalled admiration; reluctant approval of my der-ring-do; and encouragement to try for even greater prizes.

Many years later, in the company of my children, I re-mounted the big red horse with the black hooves. This time the fantasy land was called Busch Gardens. The music pounded, the horses began to fly, but it seemed ridiculous for an adult to be sitting on a little red horse with feet extended beyond the stirrups almost to the ground. And there was no ring to grab . . . and there was no one to wave to.

The world has come round many times since "zaide" waved. He is gone many years. Standing at his gravesite in Jerusalem I often conjure up the image of the carousel, and his wave of assurance. It continues to encourage me across the years.

Holidays are a time when many of us are reminded that

someone is missing. The carousel of our lives spins madly around. We are so busy trying to grab the brass ring that we do not realize what has disappeared. No one is waving. Who will shout their approval above the pounding of rhythms of our hectic lives? Who will encourage us? Who will share our victories? Who will console us in defeat?

Perhaps it is our turn to wave. Perhaps we should dismount from the big red horse and get off of the carousel. Let the next generation climb aboard. We will stand on the side-lines and wave in encouragement.

And yet—who can resist the mad whirl of life's carousel? The brass ring is just at our fingertips. Once more around and it will be ours. Don't despair. Don't give up. "Zaide" is still waving.

Gefilte Fish

Holydays evoke memories of past celebrations with family and friends. These memories become integral parts of the celebrations and are forever linked to them just as surely as the prayers and rituals. For transplanted northerners the Succot holydays present some serious difficulties: how can one be comfortable in the Succah without a heavy coat and a bowl of steaming soup with "kreplach." High humidity and uncomfortably warm temperatures just don't evoke the autumn as we New Yorkers (northerners) remember it. Although my neighbor has patented an air-conditioned Succah I doubt it has much of a future, even in South Florida.

Most important I miss my gefilte fish. No, I don't mean the canned variety that is readily available everywhere; I mean "mother's" gefilte fish, my mother's. One year she came for a visit and set out to create a gefilte fish from local sea varieties: grouper instead of white fish and snapper instead of Pike. It didn't work; it tasted O.K. but it didn't work. Gefilte fish has to have that "je ne sais quoi," those special ingredients, that secret element called "tam" in Yiddish, but untranslatable in any other language.

Finally I imported my mother together with the requisite ingredients to create a proper gefilte fish for Succot. She took out her pre-world war one handgrinder (without which you just can't get the correct fish consistency), wrapped her head in a "babushka" because no one wants to find a hair in the pot, and began to "patchka" (create).

No two batches of gefilte fish are ever the same, because the recipe changes slightly as the memory fades in and out. Essentially making fish is a process of "shitt arrein," if you will excuse the expression. It means just throw it in without regard to careful measurements. Gefilte fish is made with the heart,

213

not the measuring cup. If you need to be precise, then you belong in the chemistry laboratory and not the kitchen.

The final product needs to be cooled in the refrigerator and the fish soup ("yoch") should be jelled and served with the fish. A piece of sliced cooked carrot always garnishes the fish slice. I don't like cooked carrots and I never eat them, but I need to see that slice in the middle of my fish. It indicates that everything has been completed to perfection.

If you are a Purist you proceed to eat and enjoy. If you are like the rest of us, you spoon some horseradish ("chrain"), preferably the red beet variety, onto the fish, you cut yourself a big piece of "challa" and you begin. And with that first taste your mother is there, hovering over you, ready to serve you another helping even before you have finished the first. She can be back in New York, in Los Angeles, or even in Gan Eden, but when you take that first forkfull of real gefilte fish, she is with you.

MY MOTHER'S GEFILTE FISH

RECIPE:

5 LBS. WHOLE WHITE FISH (FILLET). (KEEP HEADS AND BONES)

GRIND FISH FILLETS AND 2 LARGE ONIONS AND A SMALL PARSNIP; ADD 2 EGGS, ½ CUP MATZO MEAL, ½ CUP WATER, 2 TBS. COARSE KOSHER SALT, 1 TSP. PEPPER, ¼ CUP SUGAR.

MIX WELL BY HAND, LET STAND AND MAKE SAUCE:

IN LARGE POT ADD HEADS AND BONES (WASHED WELL); 2 LARGE SLICED ONIONS; TWO LARGE CARROTS, SLICED; 2 TBS. KOSHER SALT, 1 TSP. PEPPER, ¼ CUP SUGAR. ADD ENOUGH WATER TO COVER ALL INGREDI-ENTS, ABOUT 3 OR 4 CUPS WATER. BRING TO A BOIL.

NOW ADD FISH MIXTURE BY MAKING VERY LARGE FISH BALLS (BY HAND). COOK ON VERY LOW FIRE (COV-ERED) 2½ HOURS. WHEN COLD REMOVE FISH BALLS, STRAIN SAUCE AND REFRIGERATE. NEXT DAY, SHABBES,

SLICE FISH AND GARNISH WITH A SLICED CARROT AND JELLED SAUCE.
   "A GUTEN SHABBES" AND "A GUTEN YOM TOV."

WITH LOVE,
   MOM

Old Friends

My two best friends are two "old" friends. They are more than twenty years my senior. My old college friends, my chronological contemporaries, have spread themselves across the country and around the world. What we once shared in common, academic interests, sports activities, social circles, have all receded into past history, along with the other common threads that bound us together. Now it is only the occasional nostalgic indulgence that animates our infrequent reunions. But our lives are no longer intertwined; we have been separated by years of separation. The understanding and empathy that is the essence of friendship is not available to people who can only share several minutes of telephone time on a birthday, or an hour waiting to change planes.

My new friends didn't share my biology laboratory, nor did they share my locker room bench. They didn't "fix me up" with a sorority pledge and they didn't walk in the procession at my wedding. Yet they share with me my immediate interests and concerns. We do not share the past, but we do share the present, and the present is where I choose to live my life.

Max was standing at the end of the pier where I was considering docking my sailboat. He had just come up from under his boat, satisfied that he had removed every last barnacle from the underside of the hull. A younger man would have hired a boat yard. In the absence of a boat yard a younger man would have been lying flounder-like on the dock, gasping for air. But Max prides himself on "staying in shape." And judging by the female shipmates who often share his Sunday sailing excursions, he is most convincing.

We adventured together: through a storm off the Florida Keys, across the Gulf Stream to Bimini, around the shoals of his family problems. The open boat was our place of communion; our psychiatrist's couch, confession box and temple of

216

meditation. We shared our hurts and disappointments, our triumphs and joys. We added our years together and benefitted from the accumulated experiences of two lives.

Was he looking for a lost son? Was I searching for a distant father? Perhaps. But who is to say what constitutes friendship.

In my presence Max is forever young. Straining to raise the thirty pounds of anchor, or scampering forward on a pitching deck to secure a flogging headsail, he testifies to his youthful vigor. He delights in challenging me, in redefining who is older. If he represents the senior citizen of the world, then I am looking forward to retirement.

According to his age, Max should be shuffling along with the legions of septuagenarians, armed with cane or crutch, marching inexorably into the night. But he has disguised himself well. He has trained all his life for this confrontation with the ogre of aging; a daily regimen of limbering up, stretching out, weightlifting, and good, hard work. He is winning the battles; and I sit at his feet studying the tactics of the master. This is his finest hour.

Chaim, my other "old" friend, is a retired executive dabbling in consulting work for a local civic organization that I belong to. If Max has age in retreat then Chaim has age out-maneuvered. Intellectually creative, agile, and incisive, he revels in problem solving. Look into his computer-screen eyes and you will see the brain waves clashing about, leaping across synapses in ever more complex patterns, tracing new thought structures in the race for answers. His brain cells are on the increase, marching in precise formation toward a better solution. He refuses to accept the equation that senility is directly proportional to chronology. He thinks, therefore he is.

A younger man possessed of such a keen mind might also project an air of superiority and intolerance. Not so Chaim. From the moment we met it was apparent that we could share our innermost concerns, without fear of ridicule, without being judgmental. We continue to advise each other on professional problems, emotional hangups, and philosophical quandaries. His advice comes from the world as it was; mine from the world as it is. We are not in competition, professionally or socially. We can take genuine delight in each other's accomplishments, feeling a sense of mutual participation and achievement.

We complement one another, pooling our experiences to equal a lifetime of trial and error learning. He can save me some of the pain; I can offer him some of the hope. Together we can find our way with a bit more confidence.

My two "old" friends have shown me the way to hobble the dragon, the one with the balding head, and the false teeth. We ride together now, partners in the struggle against aging. Along the way we have redefined the aging process. And in the process we have added new dimensions to friendship. I hope my old college friends have done as well.

A Tonsorial Trauma

"Rocco, the barber, moved to Boca Raton. Didn't he tell you?" This was my greeting when I called for a haircut. For some fifteen years my hair has been cut at the same place, in the same chair, by the same Italian barber. As with all good barbers I no longer had to give him any instructions. I could sit down and read the latest issue of *Sports Illustrated* or *Esquire* without even a furtive glance into the mirror. Rocco knew what I wanted and I had complete faith in his steady hand and practiced eye.

My son had his first haircut at Rocco's. After that first encounter with the scissors, he eventually stopped looking at Rocco as the principal in a horror film bent on removing his nose and two ears along with his hair. He is coming home from University next week and has Rocco on his list. After four months at school his hair is beyond fashionable long; but only our barber is allowed near him.

And Rocco moved to Boca Raton; and he didn't even tell us.

Sonny, the new owner of the barber shop, is anxious for our business. He assured me that he could handle the job, and I must say that his heavy Italian accent swayed me. When I found out that he came from Bay Ridge in the Italian section of Brooklyn I was persuaded to give him a try. Italians and Jews coexisted in my old neighborhood for many years. We developed a healthy respect for each other, the few incidents of youthful obstreperousness notwithstanding. We occasionally greeted each other by epithet, and sometimes the epithets were punctuated by fists. But we all held in common a devotion to our community, where the unofficial ombudsman was our barber and in whose shop many issues were settled and conflicts avoided. It is very difficult to argue with a man standing over you with a razor in his hand just inches from your jugular vein, and a barber's apron wrapped tightly around your neck barely allowing you to breathe, much less to speak.

In our neighborhood the barber had a way of imposing order on the teenage community the way the barber at Paris Island imposes order on all Marine recruits: everyone gets the same haircut no matter what you ask for. This uniformity of the top has a way of percolating down, and soon you have an element of conformity. In the Pelham Parkway section of the Bronx, Jewish and Italian kids all sported the slicked-back "D.A." look in emulation and adoration of their Italian-Jewish hero, Elvis Presley. It gave us a confidence and toughness that came up from our boots, into our black leather jackets and along our sideburns. But more important it homogenized our differences and encouraged us to consider each other as brothers instead of adversaries. This didn't prevent the occasional black eye or bloody nose, but it did serve to unite us against any perceived outside threat.

By the time I put myself into Rocco's chair, several decades had passed and a need for self expression had long since replaced a teenage desire for conformity. My hair style was an expression of "me." I liked "me," and I didn't want "me" to be changed by any attempts at creative barbering. Rocco instinctively understood this. Any attempt to suggest the slightest change had to be negotiated only after I put down the magazine, made direct eye contact and issued verbal orders. And then it would be carefully monitored through the mirror until it became apparent that barber and barbered were in agreement.

On several occasions I have arrived with a beard, usually after an extended vacation. The question is always "to shave or not to shave," and I looked to Rocco for guidance. Wisely he ignored the issue, intuitively realizing that when a man hides himself behind a mask of facial hair he must be going through some mid-life crisis relating to his job, his wife, his children, his dog, his sense of worth, his self-esteem or all of the above. I always took his Delphic approach as a sign of his disapproval; I left with a smooth chin, a recognizable face and my reclaimed personality.

Rocco is gone, along with several pounds of my hair varying

in color from light brown, to brown flecked with gray, marking my passage across mid-life. Swept away with the snips of hair are the curlicues of almost two decades of my life. But I am sure that Sonny will do just fine.

During my first visit I sat tensely, eying him in the mirror, ignoring the *Sports Illustrated* on my lap. I stepped down from the chair with a pleasing hair cut, reassured by the Bay Ridge square back, Sonny's interpretation of "leave it long in the back." He will bear some close scrutiny over the next few months, before I learn to relax again. After all, between scissors and comb he shapes my persona, and I don't allow just anyone to determine who I am.

Homecoming I

Several weeks ago I received a special invitation in the mail. It was from Yeshiva University and it requested my presence at a special convocation honoring all the Rabbis who had been granted "Semichah" in the last five years. One hundred and fifty Rabbis from all parts of the country, and indeed from all parts of the world came to participate.

It was a wonderful reunion. Notes were compared. "How are things in Los Angeles?" "Are the Jews affected by the show of French nationalism in Quebec?" "How is life in Jerusalem?"

Some of our good friends were missing. But they were occupied with special obligations. They were serving the needs of Jewish soldiers in Korea, in Japan, in Germany, and in the front lines of Vietnam.

Greetings were extended. Speeches were made.

Pride in our achievements was expressed. Pride in our Yeshiva was renewed.

But the grandest feeling of all came, not from the sentiments expressed within those walls, but from the sentiments being expressed without.

As the convocation began, hundreds of Yeshiva University's students paraded outside. Not paraded, picketed. Carrying signs. Chanting slogans. Singing songs.

But what were they picketing for? Free speech? The right to use obscene language? Free sex? The right to rule the university?

No. None of these. They were picketing for Torah. Yes, you read it correctly. For Torah. They demanded that Yeshiva University, as it enters the 1970's, be mindful of its most important goal, its most essential reason for existence. To insure the survival of our tradition.

And we thought Jewish religious identity was dying. And we thought young Jewish idealism has been misplaced.

I have been thinking about this for days. Imagine, youth so aflame with the fire of their tradition that they have made it their raison d'etre, the all encompassing purpose of their lives. So concerned for the future of our religion that they dare to take on a powerful university. A university that has hardly been challenged in all the years of its existence.

I worry about our young people. I grieve at the hundreds of souls that we lose every year, and I, with all my colleagues endeavor with all our talents, our resources and our energies to stem the tide.

It is good to see that the tide is turning. It is good to know that in this season of our "geulah," our redemption is beginning. We are coming home.

The Homecoming II

It has been eighteen years since I was presented with my certificate of "semicha" from Yeshiva University. Having duly completed the requirements for graduation, I was sent from the "Talmudic Towers" on Washington Heights out into the Jewish Community where I was expected to assume a role of religious leader, spiritual guide, psychological counselor, business administrator, executive director, consultant, architect, and a myriad other roles not included in the standard "lingua klaf" of "yoreh yoreh." Although the possibility of an extrapolation from the principles of "shechita" to those governing the dynamics of community life may not be readily apparent, there must certainly be a connection. To wit, a half dozen of my fellow classmates have successfully completed eighteen years in our chosen profession. And it was with great delight, and perhaps some trepidation that we joined at the recent Rabbinical Alumni conference to accept the honor of our Yeshiva. Delight that the Yeshiva realized that the completion of eighteen Rabbinic years is no mean feat; and trepidation that somehow we may not have fulfilled the lofty expectations of our sainted "rabbeim," most of whom watch over us only in spirit. Perhaps we wonder what they would say had they been with us on this occasion.

The day before the start of the Alumni Convention I visited the Yeshiva University campus, looking for signs of the "old days": the familiar faces, and comfortable rooms. But there were "other faces, other rooms": a new gym, its floorboards just receiving its last coat of wax, its backboards sparkling, beckoning to shoot a few baskets. A refurbished "Bet Medrash" challenging me to decipher a "tosphos." The young man supervising the new weight-lifting room reacted to my benedictions with "now we are like every other normal university." How well I remember the "old gym" and how long Yeshiva students waited to have a place where they could "crash the boards" like normal students.

Thankfully there were some familiar faces: a chance encounter in front of the dorm with my professor of English who began teaching the day I began as a University student. An equally serendipitous meeting with my first high school Talmud rebbe. A backcracking hug from our fencing coach, now ensconced in the director's chair of the new sports complex. Each encounter brought back a host of memories, many that had occupied only the nether reaches of my gray matter until now summoned forth. But the gentle face of our Rabbi Cyperstein was gone. And the Teacher's Institute office was missing the kindly countenance of our Dr. Grinstein. And the office was no longer called Teacher's Institute, or even Erna Michael. And to whom do our young students turn now in times of academic trauma, or personal distress?

The passing years have brought many changes, many for good. A new generation of our own graduates have assumed the chairs of Talmud and English literature, physics, and Jewish history. Nowhere was this more evident than via the brilliant shiur delivered by one of my classmates, and the scholarly paper presented by a fellow graduate to the assembled alumni. One hundred years after its birth our Yeshiva can be proud of its capacity for self renewal.

I often consider the history of our Yeshiva as a mirror of my personal history. Reflected upon are the careers of my father, grandfather, and uncle whose years in the rabbinate combine with mine to equal many multiples of "chai." The fourth generation of our family will soon take his place in the Bet Medrash creating a "never to be broken" tradition of commitment to the principle of "Torah and Mada."

Thus did the stream of my consciousness overflow a bit as I received my accolade from the University's senior Vice President. Certainly there are many innovations and improvements that might be suggested to our Yeshiva administration, qualitative changes that, had they been instituted in my day, would have prepared us more effectively for our "tilt with the windmill." Perhaps it is unfortunate that no one asked us (in retrospect) what we really needed. Perhaps a serious dialogue needs to be opened and maintained with our alumni, and its conclusions translated into a more relevant course of study for our students. After all, doesn't the doctor at the operating table have some interesting observations for the professor in the laboratory?

And so the "daf" turns. I and my classmates will never forget our days at Yeshiva. We were (hopefully) transformed from "sophomoric" to "semicha," more eager than ready to battle the "forces of materialism and secularism." Eighteen years later, a bit chastened, a bit wiser through experience, a bit slower from age, we are (hopefully) enthusiastically translating our Yeshiva's credo into a blueprint for Jewish communal life. We salute our Alma Mater. I am proud that somewhere in those 100 anniversary years my 18 are remembered. I am sure that every one of my classmates would, for the most part, agree.

Conquering Fear

Everyone is familiar with the oft quoted phrase, "We have nothing to fear but fear itself." But, as comforting as those words sound, we still spend a lifetime trying to conquer our fear.

Many people are never able to overcome their fears, and the best they can expect is to form a working relationship with them. A relationship that, although it will not eliminate fears, will enable a person to live with them.

Some of us are overcome by our fears. We surrender the battle and fear becomes our master. We are driven to gain artificial relief, by temporarily removing our fear, with a bottle of gin or a bottle of pills. And when the effect wears off we have solved nothing. We are plunged right back into the nightmare of our fear.

I recently read of a man who devotes his life to conquering his fear, but in a rather unorthodox manner. His name is Sam Posey and he is a racing driver.

He writes:

"I race cars because of control—the sheer joy of hurling a 200 miles an hour racing car through a steep downhill turn, the world passing in a blur, the car at the very limits of adhesion. Every lap requires an act of faith, a commitment to my skills, and the car's abilities. Every lap requires that I do something my instincts tell me can't be done. Speed itself is frightening. It is the control of the speed that is exhilarating.

"Being able to control fear—if only for a little while—is an exciting experience, one that makes me happy and proud."

We all want desperately to control our fears, and if we look hard enough we can all find our own particular method. I do not advise Sam Posey's method unless you are ready to surrender your driver's license to the nearest traffic policeman.

However, part of the answer may lie in something Sam Posey said. "An act of faith and a commitment to one's skill."

Eliminate your weakness and you shall eliminate your fears. Increase your skill and you shall reduce your fears. Believe in yourself and you will not have to fear.

Above all, have faith that in your struggle you are not alone. That there is a G-d who will never allow you to stand alone. Look for Him and He will be there, and together you shall banish fear forever.

A Purim Spiel
Presidents, Janitors and Other "Machers"

A long time ago in a synagogue far away a president was elected to office. Unfortunately he didn't know much about synagogues and even less about Judaism. But he did know something about airconditioning. So each Rosh Hashana he would ceremoniously stand up and solemnly approach the thermostat on the eastern wall of the sanctuary. There he would reverently pause to give thanks for climate control, particularly when the high holidays came out early in the heat of September. Then he would raise his hands to the controls and carefully adjust the temperature. As the giant air handler blades whispered in answer, he would slowly take three steps backward, make a circuit of the synagogue and resume his seat on the Bima.

Year after year the ritual was repeated, and each January he was re-elected to office. Heaven forfend that the oracle of air conditioning be offended by an infidel. Only the high priest of freon could be allowed to commune with the holy wind.

One day "his eminence," the President was called to his eternal reward. He had already been vouchsafed a seat near the Divine throne, or at least in a nearby airconditioning anteroom. He was even negotiating for the job of cooling down the nether world and was expecting to schedule a factfinding tour into that sultry state. He looked forward to renewing his acquaintance with the old rabbi. Hadn't the president on many occasions suggested that he go to hades, and didn't the Rabbi jump at every command?

Somehow the President lost his way. He never could find the Rabbi; and through eternity he never could stop sweating.

His eminence the president was gone, but not forgotten.

On the anniversary of his passing as the wind, his family gathered to place a memorial plaque next to the thermostat on the eastern wall. His grandson was very impressed by the comments and reminiscences of the old congregants and he resolved then and there to dedicate himself to the synagogue in the tradition of his grandfather. The airconditioning system had long since been set on timers precluding any human supervision but one electronic area cried out for attention: the microphone system. Both gigantic speakers, together with the amplifiers, woofers and tweeters, were state of the art, and when the grandson who was immediately elected president on the strength of his family connections, got up to make the announcements he was so impressed with his booming voice that I was sure he was speaking for the Lord Himself. This new president suffered from the same genetic defects as his eminent grandfather; the traditional service was foreign, therefore boring; he twisted and shifted uncomfortably in his seat for hours trying to figure out how to occupy himself until the kiddush when he could add a few ounces to his corpulence. Once at a particularly lavish kiddush he had nearly finished a whole tray of rugalach causing him to break out in a sweat and pop the shirt button just above his protruding stomach. He thought he heard someone whisper "pig'" but when he turned around no one was there, and his considerable ego automatically assumed it was a mother chastening her misbehaving children.

One day a vision came to him during the Rabbi's sermon: the microphones are never properly adjusted. From that day forward he became the chief microphone adjuster, raising and lowering the goosenecks, pushing and pulling the bases, screwing and unscrewing the knobs and nurls. As the president became more proficient and practiced he was able to fine tune the adjustments for every congregant who came up for an *aliya* and for every child who sang Adon Olam. He was so talented that he could anticipate each person's electronic needs to the nearest centimeter.

One day he needed fourteen minutes and seven different adjustments to accommodate a particularly tall congregant. His family began to worry. They consulted with a specialist who suggested that the president might have acquired the sometimes fatal Lambada Syndrome known as "microphonia," and the only known cure was immediate and total abstinence. Cold turkey.

Disconnected from his beloved microphones the president went into a depression from which even his favorite rugalach could not rouse him. He reluctantly gave up his seat on the bima; he was never seen in the synagogue again. In later years there was talk of a son who was being groomed as the new president. But no one could ever confirm or deny the rumor as the president's son never appeared in public without his radio headphones, precluding any meaningful human contact.

His candidacy was challenged by an ex-plumber who had made a study of the number of times the toilets in the synagogue were flushed during a winter Oneg Shabbat and had suggested barring all Canadian visitors in the month of February. His platform was eventually extended to include a prohibition against multiple cake eating at the kiddush unless a bona fide membership card was produced.

Be that as it may, on the fiftieth anniversary of the congregation a history of the community was published, together with the photographs of the past presidents, secretaries and custodians. No one could account for the fact that there mysteriously appeared pictures of a Rheem air compressor and a Shure omnidirectional microphone. To this very day those pictures are considered with reverence and affection, and no president dares approach the amplifier or the thermostat without offering a pledge. For what president wishes to be on the hot seat without a word to say.

Epilogue: Climbing the Mountain

My approaching fiftieth birthday began to disturb me in subtle ways. The concept of the aging process began to occupy a greater part of my daily thoughts. Articles on the medical effects of growing older caught my attention, and abstruse tracts about accumulating cholesterol and disintegrating tissues that ordinarily would receive no more than a cursory read were suddenly the objects of careful study. I had long since turned from team sports to individual competition except for an occasional "one on one" with my son or daughter. Competing against the clock, or even better, competing against myself became the new motto and I paid little attention to the fact that "myself" was not nearly as formidable an opponent as a twenty year old. Worst of all I began to feel a regular need to prove myself, to prove that everything was still in good working order, that strength and stamina were still in evidence, that age is mainly an attitude that can be modified. Neurons over biceps, cerebrum over alveoli.

The logical result of such contemplation is a movement from the theoretical to the practical. A test was in order. Could I prove that chronology was merely the confluence of numbers, five and zero to be exact, and that the true measure of the man is taken by a different set of numbers, the VO2 maximum, resting pulse and fast twitch muscles movement.

Since I have been living in Miami Beach my thoughts always turn to the mountains. The high mountains attract and excite me; the scenery delights me, and the ascent challenges me. There are few feelings that can equal standing on the summit after an exhausting and difficult climb, through snow fields and across glaciers, with crampons and ice axe. It is a feeling akin to conquering the world, or at least your personal world defined by fear, weakness and inadequacy.

Mt. Blanc is Europe's highest mountain. It straddles the

233

French and Italian border but is most accessible from Chamonix on the Gallic side of the Alps. In celebration of my 49th birthday I decided to attempt the summit at 4,400 meters. Preparations went on all year. I logged hundreds of miles on the stairmaster and treadmill, and by cycling and running around the park. A serious program of weightlifting improved my strength dramatically and careful attention to diet achieved an avoirdupois optimum. My son and training partner shared my interest if not my obsession. He had nothing to prove in the thin atmosphere of 4000 meters above sea level; rather he would be there to see to it that I didn't get into any major trouble. Jonathan and I had shared many mountains over the years, from Masada to Mt. Rainier. We have pulled, prodded and encouraged each other up some of the most forbidding terrain. We have continued on, gasping for breath, shivering with cold, on leaden feet energized only by mutual encouragement and a distaste for giving up and an embarrassment at what we deem to be unwarranted failure.

Maison de la Montagne in the heart of Chamonix provided our guide. He was half my size, his English was worse than my French, but Olivier's eyes left no doubt that he had been to the mountain, many times over. We showed up at the appointed hour at the Aiguille du Midi cable car. A tremendous thunder storm over the summit necessitated postponement. The next morning we once again slipped on our thermax underware, polypro socks, L. L. Bean wool skirts, synchilla fleeces and parkas. After struggling into our koflach boots we loaded our crampons, water canteens, granola bars and assorted gear and shouldered our packs. Ice axes in hand we tramped out of the hotel and into the dimly lit streets of early morning.

Jonathan and I were the best dressed climbing team on the mountain that day. Quietly we wondered what we had gotten into as the Aiguille du Midi cable car lifted us through the clouds and into a new world, a serious world of ice and snow and bitterly cold winds. We sat a moment to adjust our gaiters, and strap on crampons. Out came hats, gloves and "piolet" (ice axe to American climbers). I adjusted my glacier glasses and followed the route at the end of Olivier's pointing finger:

straight down an arête, falling away into a valley of snow fields, then up the wall of snow and ice to the top of Mt. Blanc du Tacul at 4000 meters. The plan called for continuing on to the top of Mt. Blanc itself but by mid day it was clear that it wasn't to be.

We roped up carefully and moved off, Jonathan in the middle surrounded by me in front and Olivier anchoring the rear in case of a slide. Our lives were in the hands of a short, skinny, Parisian window washer who looked like the next Alpine gust would blow him off the mountain. The view from the jumping off point on the Aiguille du Midi across the Vallée Blanche to Mt. Blanc was magnificent. But we would admire it only twice; before the first crampon was planted in the snow and after we collapsed at the end of the climb, with a few minutes pause in between for lunch and a photo opportunity in the Vallée Blanche before the last tortuous climb back up to the pinnacle of the Aiguille.

From the outset the terrain may be euphemistically described as challenging. Leading the team in "duck walk" through the deep snow of the arête was only the beginning. Across the valley and at the foot of Tacul we changed position: Olivier led as we moved up the slope, criss-crossing the face to deal with the ever increasing angle. At one point we looked up at a 60 degree ice wall. By driving in the toes of our crampons and the pick of our axes we laboriously crawled up, expending tremendous amounts of energy and gasping to fill our over taxed lungs. I recall becoming disoriented and using the spike of my axe instead of the top pick. The final few meters were endless, but we stood on the top. Our grins and waves of triumph are forever immortalized in that picture on my desk: Jonathan's ice axe waving in triumph and my "Leki pole" extended in victory. Suffice it to say that Olivier's casual remark that at this rate we would need another eight hours to continue to the summit of Mt. Blanc, descending and ascending twice more, convinced us that this was the time for the summit picture. We relished the moment a bit longer and then we began the descent.

Lunch was thoroughly enjoyed by Olivier, his lunch as well as ours. Cheese, bread, granola bars, raisins disappeared into the gaunt body; we could barely swallow a few pieces of chocolate. Our guide's solemn warning that we needed energy to negotiate the ascent of the final arête forced us to open another chocolate bar.

The weather suddenly turned cloudy and threatening. The sunlit vistas quickly disappeared as the wind rose and the cold intensified. Jonathan shivered in an effort to generate more body heat and Olivier rubbed him to increase warmth. Down we went, sliding on snow-packed crampons and wobbling on one foot as we attempted to knock loose the packed snow in our crampons with a sharp rap from the ice axe handle. Olivier managed to hold the end of the rope with a superhuman effort, preventing us from sliding. His constantly repeated command of "decontract Barry" still echoes in my cranium to this very day. I recall how I had no idea what he meant, thinking it was a French climbing term. When I finally realized that he was reminding me to bend my knees in exaggerated fashion in order to negotiate the steep snowy slope, things became a bit more professional.

Aiguille du Midi will always trigger a remembrance of pain, terror, and the feeling that I have stared death in the face. In deteroriating conditions we ascended the arête. The mountain dropped away steeply on both sides; a slip would carry us, or at least what was left of our bodies, all the way down to Chamonix. It was easier to deal with this precarious perch by not looking in any direction except immediately in front and down. Step by tortuous step we gained altitude. I signaled to stop; I could barely breathe. Olivier overrode me and shouted to continue. Jonathan, seized by a second wind, or a heretofore untapped reserve of energy, began to urge me on. "Just a few more meters, just a few more steps." He repeated the lie until it dawned on me that I had been fooled. But by then we were close enough for one last push.

Sitting on our porch that evening, and staring up at where we had been, I requested that I never be allowed to do that again.

We were back the next summer, this time with ultra-fuel, a secret ingredient that we were sure would get us to the top of Europe. If we could climb to the top of du Tacul, then we could ascend just a few hundred meters more to Mt. Blanc. We were wrong.

We looked great in our matching Bean checked shirts and olive green pants. Our gear was in order; but we weren't. We were just twenty four hours behind a transatlantic jet crossing; we were not yet acclimated, we were tired and nervous. Nevertheless we rode out to Les Houches with our guide and caught the train up to the trailhead. Tête Rousse was barely visible high on the mountain, our first destination in a projected two day climb. Inspecting the terrain for the first time and seeing first hand that it included a narrow slippery ledge up through the rock scree, followed by a sheer ice wall ascent, and a final approach probably shrouded in a threatening lenticular cloud served to weaken my confidence. Some three hours into the climb, after failing to overcome an oxygen deficit that kept me gasping even at a relatively low altitude, and slipping on a narrow ledge, I gave the signal to stop. I conferred with Jonathan, but I was left to make the decision. Tête Rousse was possible, but what would happen after? Climbing up an ice wall was difficult enough but what about climbing down, especially in deteriorating conditions?

We turned around and enjoyed a long glissade down the snow fields. Mt. Blanc remained in our vision, tantalizing close, but removed from us. We gave up; it was too difficult for us; there might not be another time.

Mountains are what we make of them: a pile of rock and ice, or a metaphor for life. It seems self-evident that climbing is another way of describing our movement through the physical and spiritual world, sometimes exhilarating, sometimes tortuous, occasionally epiphanous and occasionally defeating. When you have failed to achieve the summit you are forced to redefine the goal in terms of the journey instead of the destination. Actually life has no destination; it is only a journey. All is movement, and when the movement ceases so will we. We define ourselves more in terms of the struggle, not of the achievement, more in terms of how far we have come, not how far we have to go. The horizon constantly beckons, yet it will never be reached; it always remains over the horizon.

In the French Alps, in the company of a French guide from

Annecy who made the easiest four hundred dollars he will ever see for just four hours work, and with my son Jonathan as witness, I was forced to confront my age-imposed limitations. Nevertheless I will continue to test myself on the mountains. The only accommodation I expect to make is to balance desire with reality. With G-d's help the journey will progress and it will never fail to delight and inspire me. The view from the mountain is magnificent; but it only serves to remind that the next peak across the valley still beckons.